INSIDE THE MIND OF A MONSTER

A LEGENDARY CREATURE THAT DOMINATES THE MARKET

MICHEAL BURT

INSIDE THE MIND OF A MONSTER
A LEGENDARY CREATURE THAT DOMINATES THE MARKET

Copyright Micheal Burt Enterprises 2018

ISBN: 978-1-7327885-0-3

Layout and design by Navigation Advertising

First printing: September 2018

Published in the United States of America by

Maximum Success, the publishing division of CoachBurt.com

TABLE OF CONTENTS

A LEGENDARY CREATURE THAT DOMINATES A MARKET

It's my 42nd birthday and I'm listening to my family call and wish me happy birthday with these sentiments:

"You need to take time and smell the roses and try and enjoy life."

"When are you ever going to slow down?"

"Is it really that important that you push as hard as you do."

"Can't you ever be satisfied with anything?"

I'm listening to my own wife ask me this question:

"How can anyone ever help you if you want to control everything?"

I listen and think to myself.

I am smelling the roses.

I'm not going to slow down.

It is important that I push this hard toward my potential.

I am going to try and control everything, even if I can't.

This is who I am, a go hard, push every minute, unrelenting and uncompromising person who has incredible expectation first of myself and then of everyone around me. *I'm happy but I'm not satisfied.* I'm most alive when I'm creating, doing, experimenting, striving, dreaming. I hate stagnation. I hate atrophy. I hate inertia. I hate excuses. I hate whining. I'm an all in all of the time kind of person. I reward those who operate without conditions or conveniences and will do whatever it takes. I'm obsessed with the future and my potential. I only want to associate with others who have a desire and interest in their own potential. If they don't I'm out. I eliminate low value activity and those that create it.

It's my birthday and I'm frustrated. Frustrated with where I am in relationship to the potential that I have. Frustrated that we are not moving fast enough. Frustrated that I'm not on a national and international level.

But while I'm frustrated I'm also grateful and appreciative in the same moment. In the last year we've signed up hundreds of Monster Producers.

I spoke on the stage at 10X in front of 9,500 people and held my own vs. the biggest names in the world.

We are more profitable than we have ever been.

I'm getting requests to speak all over the world, including one this week in Cape Town South Africa that would pay me $55,000.

I'm hitting a stride. I'm excited. I'm curious. I want to take it all the way.

This is who I am.

I am a Monster. And I attract other Monsters, these "legendary creatures who want to dominate their markets." They feel the same way I do. They want more and are tired of others who have given up on their dreams trying to persuade them that they should slow down.

I don't want a job making under $50K with nights and weekends off. I don't want a pension and to play golf four days per week.

I want to earn millions by impacting millions. I want to be excited every day I wake up about my future. I want to matter in this world. I want to get to the pearly gates and God say, "Well done good and faithful servant." I want to eke out every talent the good Lord has given me and multiply them.

I'm content one minute and dis-satisfied the next. Confused in one moment and clear in the next. Ready to move to something bigger but trying to make sense of the demands and challenges.

This is how God wired me as a first born, type A, Leo.

I'm a Monster and my guess is if you are reading this book and either in my program or considering it you are too.

You want more.

I don't attract the mediocre.

I attract the best and brightest.

The warriors. The winners. The doers and achievers, not the floaters or blamers.

It's time you and I step up to the plate toward our calling. It's time we step in to our potential.

We don't whine. We don't complain. We don't make excuses.

We show up. We grow. We deliver.

We work the system.

We put the work in.

We let go of our amateur thoughts.

We don't listen to our feelings.

Are you fired up yet?

I am...

Now let's get this party started. If I can go from a high school basketball coach to a millionaire then you can too. I'm going to show you how to dominate first with your own thoughts and then in to your work and how you attack your day and life. I'm going to show you how to create serious impact and momentum. I'm going to show you how to dig in when you want to quit and man up when you want to give up. I'm going to show you how to "power up" when your feelings tell you to stay in bed.

I'm going to show you how "success is inconvenient" but necessary for impact.

I'm going to help you develop your hard skills so you can really impact the world in a bigger way.

I'm going to show you every MONSTER STRATEGY I have and use.

In the end only you can decide if you want to make the journey or stay where you are. Pursue excellence or pursue mediocrity.

The choice is yours.

I encourage you to push harder.

Let me start by asking you a question: *Would you be offended if someone called you a "Monster?"* I wouldn't based on the definition I use. I'd consider it a compliment.

Most of our lives, we have been taught that monsters are bad things, bad people, or something that could harm us. *But there is a new Monster*. This Monster is a person who, throughout their lives, has cultivated an arsenal of skills, talents, and experiences that when combined are used to purely dominate a market. ***They don't play, they dominate***. All of their thoughts and energies are constantly in motion. They have big engines that appear to never wonder in to a mechanical mode, but rather a barrage of actions that seem to others to never cease. They continue to dig deeper for more time, money, impact, and energy. They are the trend setters who aren't afraid to go first and take risks that others simply will not take. They attack a day vs. have it attack them and move intentionally with purpose.

Monsters are not just one of many in the field. ***They are the field.*** You might think of these people as "machines," "super freaks," "winners," or "rock stars or beasts." In my company we simply refer to them as "Monsters."

Think of a Monster as a "legendary creature who combines multiple skill sets and talents to win in ANY situation." The Monster has an "X" factor that is hard to explain or pinpoint. It's almost as if they have something in them you can't put in or you can't take out. Trying to replicate them is nearly impossible. You can emulate but you can't replicate. These people are the ones that move the world forward, advance causes, build empires, contribute millions to the economy and to philanthropy, and create change in the world for the positive.

What if we could bottle up the ingredients of a Monster and give them to you? Would that be valuable and offer you an "unfair advantage" in your market? What if sales managers all over the world could take this approach to building "Monster Producers," or if entrepreneurs could use these skill sets to build their business?

What if you could become a Monster?

Over the past 25 years I've been coaching people and do believe that we can activate the "prey drive" in another to come alive. Prey drive is an instinctual ability to see something optically and then pursue it physically. This is commonly referred to in dogs but humans have it too. Monsters have activated it. Those who are operating at nominal or ordinary levels have not found a way to activate it therefore remain in static states vs. dynamic states. They lead normal or ordinary lives vs. extra-ordinary lives. They accomplish very little vs. live the life of a Person of Interest.

This book is about the mindsets, skill sets and rites of passages you must go through to become a Legendary Creature. It's about acquiring and accumulating the necessary ingredients it takes to pivot, take action, combine skills, negotiate, relationship sell, become a *Person of Interest*, differentiate, create value, close the deal, expand, get attention, overcome obscurity, and go from a baby star to a big star. It's a book that will install an enormous amount of SWAG and self-esteem in to you.

You do want to go from a "baby star to a big star," don't you? I mean, after all, there's no better compliment in my mind than to be called a Monster. In fact, that's actually how this whole book and process began.

One day, while riding back from a coaching assignment, I asked one of my former employees this question: "What is it that you think we really do?"

If you've read our book, "Zebras and Cheetahs," you know I'm big on creating a position in the market that helps a person to clearly stand out (the Zebra) and positions them to run faster toward opportunity (the Cheetah). I also believe in becoming a "Person of Interest" that attracts massive opportunity to themselves through our book and program.

The employee looked at me and said, "Coach, do you really want me to tell you what I think you do?" I said, "Absolutely. I can't wait to hear this." That's when he said something I'll never forget.

"Coach, I think you're a freaking Monster who helps other people achieve Monster Growth in their lives and in their business," he said. "You are part 'Person of Interest,' part 'Zebra and Cheetah,' part 'Super Coach,' who combines a relentless pursuit of success with a unique ability to convince others that they have this ability too. You can sell, lead, manage, close, get attention, create opportunity, pivot, and motivate. You combine this focused approach to life, work, family, and business. You leverage your past, you leverage your skills, and you leverage your networks. You're a freaking Monster and you help take baby Monsters to big Monsters."

He finished with, "You represent the new way. The 3.0 version." Last, he added his definition of a Monster: "a legendary creature that combines multiple skill sets to dominate an area."

Bingo. We had what I am (a Monster) and what we do (we produce other Monsters).

In this book and program, I'm going to turn you into a Monster. I'm going to teach you how to combine all of the skill sets you've accumulated in your life and then add some more so that you attack the market with a flurry of intentional punches. You will never lose because you don't have the ingredients that combine to produce losses. By the end of this book, you will know what Monster Producer status looks like, feels like, and acts like.

In the same way that legendary UCLA basketball coach John Wooden had "The Pyramid of Success" and inspirational author Stephen Covey had the framework of "The 7 Habits," I have created a systematic philosophy around becoming a "Monster Producer." This model is repetitive and coordinated in my approach to helping you become the "Monster Performer" you desire to become (and will become!)

Don't be a three-toed sloth. Be a freaking Monster. What will follow will be success, money, notoriety, attention, love, referrals, reputation, and more. You're going to be distributing your talents to the world and the world is going to be distributing success right back to you.

Now, let's go be Monsters.

The 7 "Demonstrated Capacities" of a Monster Producer

With any book or program there are certain abilities that you should be gaining and mastering. In Monster Producer there are seven I think are critical to get the lift you are looking for. I am reminded of one interpretation of the "parable of the talents" in the Bible that uses the term "**demonstrated capacities**" to show *that a person has gained and used an ability, therefore garnering more abilities.* As you know I believe in "mastery" of a concept, not merely an awareness of it. To master anything you must wrestle with the concept, both in theory and in practice, until it becomes a habit. Once used over and over again with repetition you then begin to have "muscle memory" with the concept, meaning it is part of who you are. Once you have full control of a concept you begin using it with confidence. It changes and alters the results you get in significant manners and you begin to live with this mastery, making you a "legendary creature" in your market.

Here are the SEVEN core concepts one should gain during their time in Monster Producer. *Each course monthly only re-enforces one of these seven core concepts*. I believe that when you have a control of these seven concepts and are showing a "demonstrated capacity" of these seven concepts you will begin gaining the clarity and confidence you need in your business to get the lift you are looking for. Our objective for each client, who has shown a demonstrated capacity of each of these seven concepts to gain a 43% or more improvement. This will only happen through active engagement with the content, the network, and the coaching.

Demonstrated Capacity #1: The capacity to explain your services in a world class way through the E.O.S. (Explanation of Services)

The E.O.S. (created by Tom Love) helps you position yourself around what you believe and gets you out of the commodity trap.

The E.O.S. helps you compress the sales cycle, quickly ascertain who you want to partner with and forces you to articulate your value with examples and a call to action in a clear and concise manner. It is the first capacity a person should master that affects all other capacities. The E.O.S. is used in the introduction after rapport and discovery, in the follow up, and throughout the entire client interaction. It is used when sharing your message with the world to attract other people that believe the same things you do.

Demonstrated Capacity #2: The capacity to generate revenue from sufficient lead sources of qualified leads through the Legacy Selling System.

The Legacy Selling System (Burt) is a calculated and coordinated strategy of lead generation, pipeline management, and qualified lead creation. It is how a person plans and coordinates the day around the highest value of his time toward the dominant focus (a single tangible outcome to create in a 12 month cycle as measured in 30 day increments). Legacy Selling takes the chaos out of lead generation and revenue generation and brings stability to the selling cycle by placing people into sub-groups such as hit list, farm club, Top 25, Net promoters, and showcase events. This solves the problem of not enough qualified leads and time management. The Legacy Selling System is tied directly to the Monster Producer planner and should be used daily to generate leads in an effective manner and control your time. We believe in the concept of fishing for BLUE MARLINS vs. BLUE GILLS (Nagy), meaning how to think in terms of multiples vs. singles when pursing the size of opportunity one goes after daily.

Demonstrated Capacity #3: The capacity to follow up like a professional through Million Dollar Follow Up (Burt).

Most stats tell us that it takes 7-15 touches to a prospect 80% of the time to convert someone who is interested in your product or service to a buyer. The follow up system we teach focuses on "how to follow up" by using a challenger sale strategy, five steps to overcoming objection, and both linear and non-linear touches to bring a prospect to a buying decision with clarity. It also teaches how to ask great questions that re-frame the prospects thinking and establishes authority during the selling cycle. Once you have a client you need to follow up with promotion, constant engagement, and constant re-selling of the value of your services for the referral and transfer of constant energy.

Demonstrated Capacity #4: The capacity to ask for and generate referrals appropriately through promotion to existing networks, potential networks, and past networks.

The value of a network is exponentially grown by each individual participant added to that network (Metcalf's Law). We believe that every day with your current customer is an interview for your next customer and if you are getting your current client to a much better state in their lives through transformation that they will want to "advocate" for you in the market. Through the art of promotion and key techniques of conviction we teach our participants to build 25 deep and meaningful relationships, build advocates vs. passives, and ask for referrals through constant promotion and reminders of the success we are having together. We also teach our clients how to build their own power networks through events, high touch and high frequency, and unique client experiences that deepen the relationship between you and your clients.

Demonstrated Capacity #5: The capacity to attract opportunity to you vs. having to chase it by becoming a "Person of Interest" (Burt).

We believe in attracting opportunity and business vs. chasing it. *To attract others we must become more attractive* (Rohn) and this begins by garnering the seven ingredients of all people of interest. In this capacity we will go to work on the WHOLE PERSON of body (physical), mind (mental), heart (emotional), and spirit (spirit/confidence). Once we are operating at high levels in each dimension of our nature we will then go to work on likability (energy), connectivity (personality/openness), networks, and the free prize (something in addition to the product or service that differentiates. These ingredients have proven to be attractive in the market flowing power and energy to the world and coming back with opportunities in multiples.

Demonstrated Capacity #6: The capacity to become a POWER source to your networks by becoming a person of *power and influence* (POP) (Burt).

One definition of power *is a means or source for supplying energy*. We want to become energy sources for others. We believe the world is void of good energy and believe our businesses can "transform" low thoughts of value into high thoughts of value therefore changing the energy of those we interact with. When we become people who transfer this power and influence to others it builds confidence in them enabling their greatness.

Demonstrated Capacity #7: The capacity to build, grow, and scale a successful enterprises that serves our life vs. runs our life.

Being a Monster means using business to improve the lives of others and generating excess cash that can then be re-invested into future wealth building, philanthropy, and improvement for future generations, including ones own family. First we get the person to the highest level while working on the structures, processes, and systems of building successful and highly profitable businesses so the business can realize its full creative abilities and spirit. As you graduate through various levels of Monster Producer you will begin to work on the business of expansion of team, thoughts, and scale to planet Earth. We have programming for teams, the entrepreneur, operations, and other important business units that support the business.

CHAPTER 1

MONSTER FRAMEWORK #1
BUILDING A MONSTER MINDSET

"Every action you take is driven by your thoughts and your thoughts are no wiser than your understandings."
The Richest Man in Babylon, George Clason

I remember being 25 or 26 years old and going to an Achiever's Circle weekend with a small business expert named Mark LaBlanc. He would coach 10-15 small business owners, mostly speakers, coaches, and consultants through a variety of exercises devoted to helping you grow your small business. At the end of an intense three day weekend he passed the hat around the room and we put in what we thought the weekend was worth to us. I put in $500 because that's all I had to offer. Word on the street was that some of the people in the room put in $15,000.

One of the exercises was to tell the entire room what our "optimistic number" was that we wanted to generate in top line revenue monthly through our work. The guy beside me said $80,000. The other guy on the other side of me said $120,000. This was an indicator of the amount of money they were currently generating if they believed they could jump to this. When it came my turn I said, "If I could just generate $5,000 per month in coaching income" and marry that $60,000 per year with my high school teaching salary of $55,000 I would be doing over $100,000 per year. I thought to myself, "That would be awesome."

Over the past two years we have had sales months north of $500,000 in one month. Needless to say we've come a long way from then and how big my thinking was. I was a "tiny thinker" because I was hanging around other tiny thinkers. I had no one in my life who was exposing me to bigger opportunity, challenging my current thought patterns, and having conversations with me about my real potential.

To become a Monster, you must first create thoughts that are bigger than your current thought processes and this only happens when you are exposed to bigger thinkers. This is the importance of the network we are building of like minded achievers who challenge each other to expand in ways they never imagined. Metcalf's Law states, "The value of a network is exponentially grown by each individual participant that is added to that network." Our goal is to expand the network in ways that you can't imagine monthly. You should constantly be thinking of ways that you can "link" your network of clients, business partners, and friends together to grow and multiply your tribe. It increases every dimension of what you have to offer and makes your product and service increasingly valuable. It also helps to insulate yourself from competitors.

Expanding their think is hard for some because of the deep emotional and psychological scripting from their past influences. I grew up in a small town and constantly heard "you can't do that," "we are not big enough," "we don't have the resources," "that is for other people," "somebody else will achieve that but not you," and on and on and on. I got so sick of such negative subterfuge that I wrote an entire book called "Small Towns and Big Dreams" with a sub-title of "Your destiny has no city limits."

A Monster has thoughts about themselves and their businesses and their potential that are 10X bigger than they currently are and are constantly reminded that there is a gap between their current performance and their true potential, regardless of any external scoreboard. A Monster is interested in serious mind expansion and is never content or satisfied with things that are easy to achieve. A Monster is willing to meet people they have never met, go places they have never gone, try things they have never tried, and do things they have never done in order to reach their goals and aspirations.

A monster thrives on the saying Dennis Waitley shared with us in "The Psychology of Winning" when he said, "If you go there in your mind, you can go there in your body." Until you can see it and until you believe it, none of your dreams or visions or aspirations will ever materialize. You will always be limited by others' opinion of you, your own tiny thinking, or your past accomplishments.

Nobody wakes up and wants to be average or mediocre but many end up there by default. Monsters never allow mediocrity to creep into their work mode, their offices, or their thoughts because they despise being mediocre.

Remember, a Monster is *a legendary creature who combines multiple skill sets and talents to DOMINATE a market.* Notice I didn›t say, «play in the market, be one of the people in the market, or compete in the market." I said dominate!

Remember what Clason taught us in *The Richest Man in Babylon.* I break it down here:

1. Every action you take starts in the mind.

2. Every thought in your mind is only as wise as your understandings (breadth and depth).

3. Therefore, every action you take, whether small or big, is determined by the size of the thoughts in your mind.

4. In essence, little bitty thoughts equal little bitty actions, which produce little bitty outputs and returns.

I used to tell my high school basketball players "You can't put 50 cents in a dollar coke machine and get a dollar coke out." Your ability to develop a perspective that is many multiples bigger than your current framework is directly related and proportionate to these five things:

1. Your experiences

2. Your education

3. Your environment

4. Your coaches

5. Your internal drive to go beyond where you have ever been (We refer to this as "prey drive" in Monster Producer).

David Farrar, the successful basketball coach, always said, "We always want people to play within their limits, but we practice to extend those limits." I'm asking you to BLOW UP your limits and get totally unreasonable with those limits.

That doesn't just happen one day when you wake up. Many times it's inspired in us by other Monster Producers and role models who expand our limits by challenging us. Or, perhaps we experience something that awakens us to a much bigger future. The quality of the network you participate in directly affects your thoughts and size of your thinking. This is why it's vital to come in community with others on a frequent basis so you can engage with others thinking at higher levels than you.

Expanding Your Limits and Perspective to Monster Levels

There were many people who have influenced me as it relates to Monster Thinking. Two of them really stick out to me, though in different ways.

For several years, I was in Strategic Coach, an entrepreneurial coaching program which was created by Dan Sullivan. He first introduced me to "10X thinking." Just a few years later, I met Grant Cardone, author of "The 10X Rule." Both of these concepts have impacted me deeply but both come at Monster Growth in different ways and with different methodologies. From ages 18-25 I was heavily influenced by one man, Dr. Stephen Covey, the author of "The 7 Habits of Highly Effective People" and the creator of the "Whole Person Theory." You will see these influences come out through my work and in how I have built, structured, and deployed Monster Producer.

Sullivan takes you to a place in your mind where you get to pick what areas of your life are 10X greater at some future place than they are today. You may desire:

1. 10X more revenue

2. 10X more profit

3. 10X more freedom

4. 10X more impact

5. 10X more exposure

6. 10X more time

7. 10X more fun

After you pick which areas of life you want to be 10X bigger, then you step back and think "structurally" on how you would achieve this impact by making key infrastructure decisions. You may need:

1. More staff

2. More marketing

3. More accountability

4. More strategies

5. More effectiveness

6. More openness

7. More exposure to someone who is doing what you want to do

Sullivan forces you to look back in your life at areas where you have already achieved 10X results. Many are surprised to learn that they have already achieved this goal, which many believe is unattainable. That's in part because when you use words like 10X, people automatically think they have to work 10X harder -- but this is rarely the case! With a few tweaks and adjustments to your "structure," you may actually be able to exert less effort and get more yield of whatever it is that you want.

If your own business goes from $0 to $10,000 in revenue, then it grew 10X. Proportionately, when it goes from $35,000 to $350,000, it has also grown 10X. You most likely have done this already many times in your life and didn't even realize it. You need a heightened awareness to this because you already have proof of concept that it can be done (because you've done it!)

This also means it's entirely possible to do it again. There are myriad examples around you of others growing their businesses in multiples, and many of those success stories were achieved by people who are not even close to as talented as you are.

I think it's important to stop here and discuss the "biology of belief" and confidence. If you don't believe that you can achieve Monster Growth because of the past, or because of how you see rejection, or the opinion of others, or missing capital, laziness, or any other factor, then you'll never become a Monster. *You'll only take average action*. As such, you'll only get average results. And average SUCKS.

Did you know that only 8%-12% of the total population will ever break $100,000 in personal income on a yearly basis? It seems like a large number to most but then how do we explain the fact that there are also 5,220,000 millionaire households in the United States alone? That doesn't seem like such an elite group any more since it boasts more than five million people. There were over 700,000 new millionaires created in 2018 alone. If they can do it, then you can do it. I went from a high school basketball coach earning no more than $60,000 per year to a millionaire. I'm now writing a book called "Single Digit Millionaire" with a sub-title of "And how to get to double digits." Once you are worth a million dollars you will then see that you want to be worth $10 million. Imagine the life you can live, the charities you can help, the causes you can advance, and the company you can build when you create millions, or even billions of dollars of value in the market.

A study by Fidelity Investments found that 86% of today's millionaires are self-made and did not consider themselves wealthy when they were growing up. The study also found that the average millionaire was <u>61 years old</u> with $3.05 million in assets. My goal is to get you there before I did at 40 years old. I had little or no business coaching from 20-31, if any at all. *This is one of the great regrets of my life.* A good coach should accelerate your path and take off years of learning the hard way.

In my opinion, $3.05 million in assets can be achieved by YOU way before the age of 61 and in fact seems like a small fortune in comparison to those possessed by some of the truly Monster Producers in the world. I guarantee you that those people don't have anything that you don't have -- except perhaps some Monster thinking and Monster confidence! We have people in Monster Producer now that earn upward of $4 million in personal income and they don't own massive companies. They just had a "long obedience in the same direction" and have put in the time to take control of a concept and master it.

I believe confidence is the ONE thing that affects everything. It is either the great enabler or the great disabler of your success. It is either your greatest asset or your greatest liability. **Monster Confidence** could be described as:

1. The memory of success

2. The ammunition you need to achieve Monster status

3. An internal knowing you have that allows you to create what you see in your mind

Think of it this way. You are not "chasing success." You are merely pursuing your own internal vision of what you see in your mind's eye. If you see something small, then you act in small ways. The belief and confidence you create is vital to achieving Monster Growth. As you pursue a dominant focus with a laser like mindset you will ascertain the control you need to attract all kinds of new opportunity to you. My philosophy on selling is simple: Money changes hands when problems are solved. The bigger the problem the more money people will pay to solve it. Be a world class problem solver and you'll earn some MONSTER MONEY.

Many years ago, a good friend of mine named Rick Kloete told me that he could find a four-leaf clover ANYTIME and ANYWHERE that he wanted to. He said he knew he could do it, and because of that belief he could go out on any morning while drinking coffee and find as many as 16 four-leaf clovers in ONE morning. *This is confidence.* This confidence comes from his "demonstrated capacity" of doing it over and over again. He also noted that most people never even look for a four- leaf clover because they immediately say, "I'll never be able to find one." They never start because their mindset is plagued from the beginning by a lack of confidence. Saying you will never be a millionaire and believing it's only reserved for others and not yourself if the problem of most people.

Who is coaching you matters. Over the last seven years No one has helped me to cultivate a bigger sales mindset than megapreneur and good friend Grant Cardone, founder of 10X and owner of almost a billion dollars of real estate. His books and various programs focus on 10X as an action, not just a structure. Whereas Dan Sullivan of Strategic Coach™ challenged me to think in terms of building a structure that would allow me to achieve 10X results in any area of my life, Cardone challenged me to think in terms of taking 10X action to achieve that success.

These are two different mindsets but both are directly tied to the Monster Producer and the mindset of growth we are trying to achieve with this book and program. In my mind, you must combine Sullivan's challenge with Cardone's vehicle and motivation to get yourself from point A to point B on the road to success.

An example of Cardone's Monster Thinking would be where he defines the four levels of action:

1. Do nothing

2. Retreat

3. Normal

4. Massive

His strategy revolves around 10X your goals, your actions, your movement, your strategies, and your efforts. To become a Monster Producer, here are seven specific strategies you need:

1. Sit down and write out today what your company would look like in multiples of five times greater in these areas:

    a. Revenue

    b. Profit

    c. Size

    d. Number of employees

    e. Offices

    f. Offerings (We believe you should have multiple offerings to pivot to in the sales cycle)

2. Sit down and write out today what areas of your life you want Monster Results in:

    1. Money

    2. Freedom

    3. Exposure

    4. Opportunity

    5. Leads

    6. Profit

    7. Health

3. Sit down and write out the five new strategies you are going to use to achieve these results:

    1.

    2.

    3.

    4.

    5.

4. Sit down and write out the three new places you want to visit to expand your mind (think places where you would be exposed to something powerful):

    1.

    2.

    3.

5. Sit down and write out the five people you would like to meet that would offer you a bigger mindset:

    1.

    2.

    3.

    4.

    5.

6. Sit down and write out the five big experiences you would like to have or would like to attend where you would get to see world-

class people perform (This could be a conference, opera, concert, learning event, etc.):

1.

2.

3.

4.

5.

7. Now, sit down and write what your life looks like five years from now as a result from this Monster Thinking:

Hello I'm_____years old. I live in a_____ house in this city. My company, which is_____ now produces _____the amount of revenue it used to with a profit margin of_____. My investments are making me_____per year and have me on track to produce _____by age_____. My personal annual salary is _____ and I have been able to _____, _____, and _____ _____ because of this income. My business is now self-supporting and I only work_____hours each week. I get to take_____days off per year. Since becoming a Monster Producer over the last five years, I've been able to cross several things off my bucket list, including _____, _____ _____, _____, and_____. The only thing left to do now is _____.

I also now get to spend _____ of time pursuing _____
_____ and my family and kids are able to enjoy
_____ because of my Monster Mindset.

Remember, if you go there in your mind you can go there in your body. Many will never even be able to muster the positivity to go there mentally, therefore they check out physically. As a consequence, they just stay at their current (and mediocre) production levels. In Monster we believe that your drive to move toward your dominant focus must be so strong that is overcomes your drive to stay where you currently are.

Creating a clarity of thought is vital to be a Monster. It helps you eliminate CONFUSION which could be classified as:

- Randomness in motion

- A problem or complexity that appears to have no clear or immediate solution

Most people attack their days around this confusion and it looks like randomness in motion.

To eliminate this in Monster Producer you will need:

- A clear dominant focus, which is a single tangible outcome you would like to drive in a 12 month cycle as measured in 30 day increments (Notice I said "tangible focus" that can be measured by units, volume, or time)

- An "Explanation of Services" which will help you articulate what you believe, what you do, and a call to action. This will be a small hinge that turns the entire door in everything we do.

- A selling system to drive leads and opportunity and attack a day. Where there is no system of lead generation there is "randomness in motion."

- A follow up system to bring prospects or opportunity to a close. We teach a concept called "Million Dollar Follow up" that shows how to follow up appropriately and trigger a buying decision.

- A strategy to promote to your current clients to extract 4-6 referrals from every interaction after you get your clients to a much better state.

- A strategy to become a "Person of Interest" to attract new opportunity to you vs. chasing by going to work on key ingredients you possess that drive up your attractiveness in the market.

- A strategy to become a "Person of Power" as a supply source for new energy to others. The world is void of energy and those that consistently put out enthusiasm become power sources for others.

- A strategy to build, scale, and grow your enterprise so it makes money whether you are there or not and you can play in your unique skill zone.

Imagine for just a minute building something that looks like this:

- A business that you see simply as *a game and revenue source* for all of your future growth vs. a business of *confusion and anxiety*.

- That business allows you to work with and control your own unique talents daily and work with others who deeply value those talents and compensate you at the highest levels for those talents vs. a business that places you in low value activities that drain your energy.

- A business that gives you *excess cash at the end of every month* that you can then re-invest in future endeavors and wealth building as part of your legacy.

- A team of like minded people who help you build, maintain, and protect your confidence and give you energy vs. drain your energy. These people believe in you and your mission as much as you do vs. uneven levels of commitment.

- A business and enterprise you love to go to daily and can't wait to fulfill your creative spirit through the distribution channel of that business.

This is possible when you get your mind right and these are the precise things we will be working on with you in Monster Producer. Now let's go to work on your skills to advance.

CHAPTER 2
MONSTER FRAMEWORK #2
DEVELOPING THE "MONSTER SKILL SET"

A Monster not only has knowledge, he has impeccable skills that have been honed and refined over many repetitions. It is his skills that give him the ability to be compensated at the highest levels of interaction. We believe in spending 10 years developing one HARD SKILL SET. This is a skill set that solves a problem in the world. Once this PRIMARY skill set is developed it can then be used to generate income and intentional congruence (secondary flows of income that open new revenue sources).

How to build a Monster skill set that combines multiple abilities into one hybrid approach that is agile and differentiated

While preparing for my presentation at the 10X Growth Con in Las Vegas to 10,000 people Grant Cardone asked me to walk the audience through my story of starting as a high school basketball coach turned entrepreneur and ultimately a single digit millionaire. He wanted me to talk the audience through "inflection points" from when I earned $60,000 per year as a coach working 80 hours per week to earning over a million per year as a coach and entrepreneur. This forced me to "codify" my journey and my key moments.

In the first working decade of my life (15-25 years old) I did one thing: developed a "hard skill" that would help other people learn to perform at a higher level. This hard skill could be called "coaching." I spent over 10,000 hours honing and refining this skill until it was world class. It would be the reason people still compensate me to this day.

In my second working decade (25-35 years old) I also learned how to sell, solve problems, promote, negotiate, articulate, and build deep and entrenched networks. These would be "secondary skills" to my "primary skill." This showed me the problem for millions of people around the world. They didn't have a "hard skill" that could be used to solve problems for others and their primary skill wasn't strong enough to "stack" other skills on top of to earn more and more money.

Know this, until you have a hard skill that solves a big problem you'll never earn a lot of money. Remember, money only changes hands when problems are solved. The Monster cultivates a hard skill first and then learns secondary skills to advance the primary hard skill.

Last week while speaking to an investors group in Raleigh, NC I explained to them this cycle:

1) I developed a hard skill of coaching

2) I then created a network of people who wanted that skill

3) After developing the network of over 600 I then figured out that roughly 16% of those people are big time people with money and resources

4) I could then go to the top 16% (Typically the $25K and above members) and form partnership, raise capital, and start new businesses

5) We could then partner to purchase and invest in real estate

I reminded them that I wouldn't have a network of 600+ if I first didn't have a hard skill that solved a problem for them. This was the beginning of me building a network of exchange.

Developing your hard skill is vital to become a MONSTER.

Many years ago, you could win with one skill set -- or what some called a "trade." You went to work and performed that skill all day every day and the company compensated you for that "one skill." It is true that you can earn a good living by knowing and controlling one skill but building a business may require you to hone multiple skills along the journey.

Before we can build a secondary skill set the Monster must find, hone, nurture, and refine a primary skill set. This is what I call a "hard skill." Think of it this way, your unique talent once refined over a long period of time becomes incredibly valuable to solve a problem for someone else. If that problem is big enough you are rewarded with bigger paychecks (something we call Blue Marlins in the program). Until you have a primary "hard skill" you are just a commodity, meaning people believe they can get you anywhere. If the consumer believes they can get you anywhere why would they pay more money for you? They wouldn't.

You get yourself out of the commodity trap by developing this hard skill set and then become known or famous for solving certain kinds of problems in the market place. As your status gets higher and higher you become a "person of interest," the fifth concept we teach you in Monster Producer.

The development of my hard skills began as early as six years old when I was directing, leading, encouraging, and maturing as a young baseball player. Even then my coach Micki Vinson, a female little league coach said to me, "Son, one of these days you are going to be a great coach." I would go to work nurturing, refining, and expanding this concept of coaching over the next 35 years of my life to where I am today. Once you have a general "hard skill" that skill will become more apparent and finely tuned. I would now tell you that my hard skills are:

- Associating concepts into packaged ideas that get people to think, move, or take action

- Taking complicated growth concepts and making them simple and easy to understand

- Delivering concepts with a cadence and conviction that inspire people in their own lives

- Transferring a "contagious confidence" and belief system to others in a way that builds their self-esteem

Now the question becomes "what problem do these skills solve" and "who would pay me to solve them."

I tell my team all the time that we solve these problems:

- Confusion
- Confidence
- Lack of structures
- Insecurity
- Focus
- Motivation
- Energy
- Networks
- Systems

I began developing these "mental constructs" as early as six years old and they have been fueled by the books I've read, the conferences I've attended, the coaches I've hired, and the relationships with successful people that I've built.

I then have to ask myself, "How do we sell these solutions in bulk to millions of people?" This is where the real money is.

Now, I'd like to ask you these questions:

1. What is your "hard skill?"

2. What problem does it solve?

3. How did you develop it?

4. Who would write you a large check for it?

5. What makes it different than others in your field?

6. What are you doing to work it and refine it?

Until you have this you can't leverage it into a concept you will learn later called "Intentional congruence," which is where you tie concepts and money generating mechanisms together through the leverage of your primary and ultimately your secondary skill sets.

The Industrial Age ended and people began to figure out that they had four things the world needed:

1. Knowledge (for the mind)

2. Skills (for the body)

3. Desire (for the heart)

4. Confidence (for the spirit)

They no longer could get by using one skill. This is why Monster Producers combine "multiple skills" to dominate a market. In a given day I may be:

- A psychologist solving internal confidence issues

- A motivator keeping people in a forward posture

- A sales person articulating concepts to bring people to a buying decision

- A creator of content to push out to the market to drive up my "Person of Interest Score"

- A problem solver dealing with my own employees and how to create better processes

To be a Monster you can't be ONE DIMENSIONAL early on. Later as you begin to build the systems and processes and team members around you it will then be possible for you to refine ONE HARD SKILL in which you are compensated at the highest levels. Early on you will be the chief, cook, and bottle washer. This is an important aspect of becoming a Monster that will appear overwhelming at times. There will be a confusion of time, money, and next steps. All of this is perfectly normal. Don't allow this to cause you to quit or contract (something many people do). Remember, Monsters use FEAR as

FUEL. Average people use FEAR to debilitate. You are not average if you're in the Monster Producer coaching program.

Over time your skill set needs to evolve and become multi-faceted with an ability to adapt and adjust in varying environments. You need to be able to sell yourself and your product or service, solve complex problems, add immediate value to a company or prospect, and create assets vs. become a liability. In essence you will find out two important things:

1. You needed multiple skills to WIN in a global economy and those skills needed to evolve

2. Your skills are transferable across various mediums (you just didn't know this until now)

At 25 years old I wrote my first book and I wrote it for coaches. The unintended positive consequence of writing that book (an action) was that business people began to purchase my book and ask me to speak (something I didn't expect). They began compensating me at a rate of 10X greater than I was making in the athletic coaching arena. It was then and over the next few years that I saw a much bigger future as an entrepreneur (a person who takes lower level resources to higher levels of productivity). I saw myself as a global motivator and America's coach, not just a local basketball coach. But it was the studying and the skills I had acquired while building a championship program that prepared me for the multiple skills and confidence I would need to win at the highest levels in business.

Remember the definition of a Monster which is a "legendary creature that combines multiple skill sets and talents to dominate a market." When I was a championship women's basketball coach, I worked hard to cultivate a valuable skill set that combined:

1. How to gain insight into how teams worked or, alternately, become dysfunctional

2. How to coach and develop the whole person

3. How to bring business and entrepreneurial thinking into the sports arena

4. How to get buy-in both as a leader and of my system

5. How to negotiate power plays and struggles

6. How to build high levels of trust and influence

7. How to solve complex problems that involve emotional intelligence

Then one day I asked, **"Who else would pay for these skills that I've accumulated?"** You should be asking yourself this question that we remind our Monsters of monthly. This is a question I learned from Dan Sullivan:

What is the largest check that you have ever cashed and where did it originate? And, why haven't you gone back there and found another one?

In Monster Producer we refer to these as ***BLUE MARLINS vs. BLUE GILLS***. My good friend Scott Nagy, who built and sold a company for millions by the time he was 40 years old said to me one day, "Coach, you and I are both fishing. The difference is that you are fishing in your local lake for blue gills and I'm fishing for blue marlins in the gulf of Mexico."

This piece of advice will come in handy when we begin to discuss the selling system and your hit list, key targets that you want to get in front of to share your services with who you believe you can "help."

It turns out that many entities beyond my basketball squad wanted to take complexity and make it simple -- especially as it related to Monster Growth. People are obsessed with progress, growth, change, achievement, stretching, and winning. All I had ever done in my life was study these things and practice what I had learned! I realized there was a whole new world willing to pay for my solutions to their problems, the value I could create in their organizations, and the unique processes I had cultivated that could right their ship!

Remember: Money changes hands when problems are solved. The bigger the problem the more money people will pay to solve it. Your talent (which I believe is God-given is used to solve their complexity). You are then compensated in the form of love, money, recognition, referrals, and reputation.

You most likely have various skills that you've never "packaged" into a skill set and sold. They may be disconnected and are most likely under-valued by you. *That's not the world's fault, it's yours*. It's your job to do three things:

1. Find your "special" - that combination of skills, talents, and capacities that the world needs

2. Package your special - take your intellectual property and package it in a consumable way

3. Sell your special - get exposure for what you've got

While trying to get attention for a new book I had written through a reality TV show called "Zebras and Cheetahs" I highlighted exactly how to do this. In it, I coached five people over the course of two grueling days and three difficult challenges to find out what makes them unique in the world, to teach them how to package that uniqueness in the form of words, frameworks, marketing collaterals, and position statements, and finally how to pitch and sell that "special" to a board of directors. Every person who appeared on the show has said this process forced them to dig deep into their tool shed of skills and talents to clearly differentiate themselves amidst a noisy and saturated market. But what if you never have those grueling two days of refinement? You just continue to do what you've been doing.

The Monster Producer must understand that like a *Swiss Army Knife* that combines twelve different functions in a single knife, they too must develop a skill set that is so valuable, so differentiated, so multi-faceted, and so imperative that the world will compensate them in the form of massive returns in exchange for gaining access to it. Many I coach never even dig in to their skill sets and who would compensate them at the highest levels for those skills. They never find their first and primary "hard skill" to then "stack their skills on top of each other" to become valuable and versatile in multiple situations. This leaves them lacking in value which means they are going to be lacking in their bank account. Without a hard skill you will be stuck in an occupation doing low level work that will appear meaningless. To get in the big games of life you need hard skills that solve real problems. If those solutions increase the revenue for others then they won't mind sharing a little "piece for your niece" as my good friend Brad Lea (founder of Lightspeed VT) says.

In my opinion, the most valuable skill sets in the world that are the most rewarded financially today are:

1. Critical thinking and problem solving (Money changes hands when problems are solved)

2. Active listening with solutions to follow (But also "associating concepts" that carry over from one arena to another)

3. Complex judgment (The ability to see and deal with multiple things at one time)

4. Time management (The ability to eliminate time confusion and stay focused on the prize which is generating new income and solving big problems)

5. Sales (Maybe this should be #1)- A minimum of two hours daily of prospecting for new money.

6. Writing (You will need to be able to speak, coach, write, and articulate)

7. Speaking (Monsters get in front of groups and "batch" events together to reach more people. This will require more from you).

8. Management of resources (How do you multiply time and money in big ways) This will include overcoming fear in your

mind of losing money but rather spending money to "flow" new opportunity

9. Development of human capital (How do you move from a solo-preneur to an entrepreneur who owns a business vs. runs the business)

10. Ability to turn liabilities into assets (Take lower thought of value and convert it to higher thought of value)

11. Ability to see and seize or create opportunity (Again, selling is solving problems. The Monster goes in to the market and looks for opportunities to create revenue by solving bigger and bigger problems)

While speaking to a group of college students one time, investment guru Warren Buffet once offered "$10,000 as an investment in your future," but added that "if any of you are great public speakers, I'll give you $150,000." Why would Buffett say such a thing? Why would he place such an inflated value on a relationship with an effective speaker? He did so because communication is valued at a high premium in the world and because it's a form of packaging and articulating what it is you possess, what it can do to improve the world, and why the consumer needs it. The Monster Producer excels at packaging their skill set in a crystal clear way around their position, content, differentiated skill set, and the clarity they have to offer to the world.

I like to break it down and make it simple. The Monster Producer at an *entry level* needs to be able to do at least these four things to be viable in the market and be what we call "An immediate asset"

1. Add some type of immediate value. People no longer have time to "coach up" new talent and wait for long cycles of return. You need to walk in on day one and create immediate value.

2. Sell something, including yourself, both internally and externally. Selling is the exchange of money for value and price only becomes an objection in the absence of value.

3. Fix the biggest problems the company or prospect is currently experiencing. Companies biggest problems today have to do with sales and fulfillment (operations). Culture is also a major issue for many.

4. Become an "immediate asset." Never forget that assets add time, money, energy, or invisible assets while liabilities subtract time, money, or energy. Too many cost time and energy with low value thinking, lack of preparation and overall laziness.

I want to expound a bit on this last one, and build off of it as well.

In my book "Zebras and Cheetahs," we introduced a phrase we termed "the current of the urgent." This was symbolic of the Class Five Rapid of time management that people in this day and age are swirling in. The Monster Producer builds a valuable skill set in a way that they can pitch it and sell it and produce results in 20 minutes or less. The world simply doesn't have time for a long cycle to show a return on an investment. The Monster Producer walks in and immediately creates value from the very beginning by raising the energy, raising the stakes, and raising the effort level and the bar of everyone around them.

To more fully understand this "Immediate Asset" skill set, you need to go back to the old Dale Carnegie days of "How to Win Friends and Influence People" so that when others are with you, *they feel better about themselves.* You raise the playing field for everyone. To do this, you must always be considered an asset v. a liability.

Think of assets and liabilities in this way. Assets feed me. Liabilities eat me. Assets add time, energy, and money, or save one of these things. Liabilities subtract.

There is, however, an asset you can win with that never shows up on a profit and loss sheet. This is called an "invisible asset" or "intangible asset." This is where the Monster Producer thrives because he cultivates these skills in addition to the hard skills he already has.

Invisible assets Monsters possess could include these 20 that are effectively combined in order to dominate:

1. Focus

2. Drive

3. Ambition

4. Trust

5. Likability

6. Relentless pursuit

7. Bounce back

8. Connectivity

9. Penetrating knowledge

10. Chemistry

11. Intense understanding of an area

12. Freakish work ethic

13. Ability to fit in or stand out

14. Ability to pivot while selling

15. Large retention skills

16. Ability to combine information not related

17. Ability to pull and extract information and use it

18. Instant recall

19. Unwillingness to accept no or give in

20. Ability to will and convince others of a bigger future

Combine this skill set with the basic four I mentioned earlier…

1. Body = Skills

2. Mind = Knowledge

3. Heart = Effort

4. Spirit = Confidence

…and now you have a Monster.

You may already have many of these skill sets. The tricky part is drawing them out of the closet and putting them on the street so the world knows you have them and that they are valuable. Once the world knows you have them and they are valuable, only then do you begin to get compensated at the highest levels with love, money, recognition, referrals, and reputational capital. This is when you begin to distribute your skills to the world in a way that the world recognizes.

Now the question becomes: how do I build this arsenal of skills so that I can deploy them at a moment's notice?

Many people spend years accumulating these skills in the hopes of one day utilizing them but they never get fully compensated for their value because their packaging is weak and commoditized. As long as the world sees you as a commodity, you'll never become a Monster. That's because there are simply too many choices of others who are perceived to be capable of doing exactly the same things that you do. The packaging of these skills and the execution of them is where the real players dominate.

Here are some methods for building a stronger tool shed:

1. Find and fill your "missing structures." A missing structure is a void, gap, or hole in your skill set that if filled could have you sitting on "acres of diamonds." We all have missing structures. You must do a full autopsy on yours. I've found that many "baby monsters" lack connectivity or likability and are in the business of turning

people off v. turning them on. This one missing structure could kill all of your momentum toward becoming a Monster Producer.

2. Develop the ability to extract, internalize, and deploy large amounts of information. The Monster is constantly studying the work of all the greats but also has an uncanny ability to extract key facets from other people's intellectual property and adapt it in a way to help them win. For example, *Rich Dad Poor Dad* author Robert Kiyosaki never talks about "immediate assets" in any of his works and rarely talks about people as assets or liabilities. But I extracted that meaning from his work and used it in a new context to articulate a point. Just as baking soda was once used exclusively for baking purposes, but is now also used to deodorize a room, you too can "riff" off the thinking of others to help find and crystalize your unique message. It's the same product just used in a new context. Monster Producers don't just go to classes and read books, they DEVOUR the content, internalize it, retain it, and deploy it for a competitive and unfair advantage. They get what others who are too lazy to do it never will.

3. Make a habit of spending time with talent. Part of the Monster's selling system is getting embedded with weekly "talent searching" to grow their skill sets. People get complacent. They hang out in comfort ponds. The Monster never gets complacent or disengaged but actively seeks out the best in every industry and finds a way to glean pearls of wisdom from each of them. They hunt down great people and spend time with them as part of their weekly regimen.

Packaging Your Monster Skills into Assets that Make Money

One of the biggest challenges of "baby monsters" is their packaging. They've got million-dollar brands and fifteen-dollar packaging. How you package up the Monster skills you've acquired is critical to commanding top dollar in the market.

Think of packaging as any tool you can use that the market sees. Your e-mails are packaged. Your marketing collaterals are packaged.

Your website is packaged. How your office looks is packaged. How you dress is packaged. Your social media is packaged.

To better understand this, we must first pick a clear position in the market based on your skills. Your position should tell us why we should have a relationship with you in a clear and compelling way.

Here are some examples of poor packaging:

1. Coach

2. Speaker

3. Banker

4. Real Estate Agent

5. CPA

None of these articulate anything but "I am a commodity." By contrast, what we want to do with our skills is articulate them in such a way that people will instantly know who you are, what you do, and how you do it differently from other people.

For example, I always refer to myself as a "Super Coach" who combines a former championship coach with an entrepreneurial mind. This says I know how to win (important for those who are serious about winning) and how to run a business (entrepreneurs take lower-level resources to higher levels of productivity).

There are millions of coaches. There are millions of speakers, bankers, agents and accountants. Monsters package themselves in novel ways that people can identify with quickly and they do it with evocative language and phraseology that people are attracted to.

Here are a few examples. After reading them, I want you to focus on your position statement (or what I commonly call your "Zebra Statement).

'Hi, I'm Coach Burt and I'm an entrepreneur who specializes in doubling the amount of profit you make in half the time anybody else can do it.'

OR

I help eliminate any confusions you might have both personally and professionally so you can achieve a 43% increase in one year.

Does this get your attention? BAM. How about…

'If you want more profit (and who doesn't?!?!?), then I am your guy.'

This is so much better than speaker, coach, author, radio and TV host, etc. (This one is actually a packaged position statement I heard from another person and it immediately got my attention.)

Your position starts by understanding what makes you unique in the market and is then spread across all the mediums at your disposal to articulate that "special" so people know they need exactly what you've got!

The reason you need to know and combine the skill sets of a Monster is that in today's world people need agility. They need to know you have an arsenal of tools in your tool box to help them achieve the results they want. The old days of possessing just one skill set are over because market forces have changed. Just like a sports player can no longer just do one thing well and expect to get on the playing field, you can no longer just have just one skill and expect to be a go-to person in the business world! It is the combination and synergy of multiple skills that makes you attractive to the market.

Many will tell you to specialize in order to dominate a market. I don't entirely disagree; but how you really dominate is by using various skills packaged together into one person or firm that makes you attractive.

Here are some questions for you to begin thinking about as it regards your skill set:

1. What is it that you really do? Don't write down the title but rather the action and the outcome.

2. What makes you better at doing it than anyone else? This will come from your unique past and leveraging your skill sets. No two pasts are the same. Your past is what makes you unique.

3. What unique knowledge have you acquired (and from whom) and how does that give you an unfair advantage in your market? This typically comes from "how you see what you see." You may have a unique skill set at seeing something as an asset vs. a traditional liability.

4. If you had to combine your top three skills, what would they be?

5. When you really look at your "missing structures," what are they and what are you willing to do to fill them?

6. Name the top 3 competitive advantages you believe you have in your market.

7. Write out the top 3 skills of three Monster Producers you admire in your professional space.

8. Write out your new position statement explaining why people should have a relationship with you based on the combination of skills you have.

Packaging your services through the Explanation of Services

For over six years now I've had a great relationship with Tom Love, the creator of the E.O.S. Tom had the genius to combine multiple concepts into one framework for explaining your services by watching and synthesizing these concepts:

- My book "Person of Interest" about becoming a must have vs. a nice to have and only looking for people who are looking for you

- Simon Sinek's book "Start with Why" and popular TED TALK

- The book "The Challenger Sale"

From these three concepts and Tom's successful career in the insurance profession he created a framework that would change how people share their beliefs with others that we adopted in Monster Producer.

We believe that people do business with other people who believe the same things they do. Because of this belief selling is really just partnering with others to solve a problem for them that believe the same things you do.

In our program one of the first things we focus on is how you explain what it is you do to keep you from the dreaded commodity trap many find themselves in.

We also believe that "having something to say is just as important as having somebody to say it to." Many go out in to the world and say the same things that others have.

We teach the E.O.S. this way:

1. First get clear about what you believe (this is based on finding your WHY). Once clear then begin to share your beliefs with others to see if they believe what you believe (you should know in the first 15 seconds if you do this correctly). Pick up a copy of Sinek's books "Find your Why" and "Start with Why."

2. Second, share with others why you believe it (support your premise).

3. Third, tell me what you actually do (keep it incredibly simple but to the point and specific).

4. Fourth, explain one to three ways in which you do it differently than others in your space.

5. Fifth, give me some social proof of you doing it for others with an example.

6. Sixth, ask me a question, "If I could do this for you like I've done it for these others what would stop us from moving forward?"

This E.O.S. could also be broken down into just three critical steps:

1. Offer a statement of belief.

2. Cite an example of what you have done for someone else.

3. Give me a call to action.

Here's an example of my E.O.S.

I believe "Everybody needs a Coach in Life."

I believe that because you can't see the picture when you're inside the frame and those that have a coach earn 3-4X more than those that don't.

Because of that belief I've created a structure called Monster Producer, which is an ongoing and consistent coaching program designed to help you get a 43% increase in year one with me.

The real difference in our program vs. others is the live component as we offer 3-5 live trainings per month, two weekly rhythms, and up to two special courses as well on key parts of our system. We help you find and fill your missing structures which are typically these.

We currently have over 585 people in our program with a goal to get to over 1,000.

If we could get you a 43% increase in your sales what would prohibit you from coming to experience the energy and exchange next month?

It's time for you to go to work on your E.O.S.

1. What do you believe:

2. Why do you believe it?

3. What do you actually do for your clients?

4. How do you do it differently than anyone else in your industry?

5. Cite one example or multiple examples of who you are doing it for.

6. Ask the key question to get started

This is critical for a number of reasons:

- This is a process of clarity for you

- You won't be able to market or brand yourself until you have clarity about these things

- You won't have anything valuable to say until you work this out

- This clarity tells you who you want to partner with and who you don't

- You don't want to enter in to partnerships with others that don't believe the same things you do

Serious professionals go to work on their explanation of services. Amateurs don't. Amateurs remain in a commodity trap. Professionals separate themselves from everyone else by how they articulate their unique value. Go to work on this from the beginning as it will affect every component of how you build your business, who you hire, how you follow up, and more.

CHAPTER 3

MONSTER FRAMEWORK #3 "TAKE MONSTER ACTION STEPS"

Monsters commit first and allow their creativity to follow. They do not get caught up in perfection which paralyzes them

Part of being a Monster is taking "Monster Action" — but not just any action.

We must align our time with the highest and best use of that time. Then we must marry it to our top strategies in order to progress toward our dominant aspiration.

We really need Monster focus coupled with a willingness to do the inconvenient things that others are not willing to do in order to make it happen.

Most people take normal levels of action. Very few take massive levels of action. In addition, the biggest challenge for many people is that even if they take lots of action they almost exclusively devote it to very low-level activities. By contrast, Monsters use strategies and steps in key areas that leverage their actions to multiply their future faster.

Rather than just be busy for the sake of being busy (and getting very little in return), this chapter is about gaining clarity about the Monster Action steps that you can take to multiply your future. Those who have for instance achieved 10X their company's revenue numbers many times over took tangible steps that yielded such Monster results.

Let's start by understanding that all of this action is aimed toward one thing: our dominant aspiration. **This is a single, tangible outcome you would like to drive in a 12-month cycle as measured in 30-day windows**. Technically, it could be an intangible; but you really need some way to measure and track activity toward this aspiration on a weekly and daily basis.

Once we know what our dominant aspiration is then it will become clear every day (and in every way!) that we are either taking action that is in alignment with that aspiration or it is not. It's so easy to let low-value activity creep into your schedule and exhaust you when if you just stepped back and realized you were doing this you could stop the regression and instead get your focus back on activities that multiply your future and add kerosene to the fire you are building! Think of these actions as multipliers.

In a given day you will hear me say "Focus on your high value activities." Remember, HVA's are specific, intentional activities that move you closer to your dominant focus. A "Low value activity" is an activity that you participate in that moves you "away" from your dominant focus.

High Value Activity could be defined by doing these things:

1. An intense and focused effort on NEW MONEY daily or MONEY GENERATING ACTIVITY

2. An intense effort to get your current clients to such a better state by becoming an asset to them that they bring you new clients through deep advocacy and referrals

3. An intense effort of promotion to become a "Person of Interest" where you are attracting large numbers of people to you (For every 30 people you get in front of only 4.8 will be interested in your services). Most people do not do a good job of promotion therefore only marketing to a small number of people.

Remember, a DOMINANT FOCUS is **a single, tangible outcome you would like to drive in a 12-month cycle as measured in 30-day windows**

Now it's time to come up with yours:

My Dominant Aspiration is _____

_____

My top five Monster Action Steps to drive this aspiration are:

1. _____

2. _____

3. _____

4. _____

5. _____

Amateurs think. Amateurs discuss. Amateurs study. Amateurs wonder. Monsters ACT! They don't get caught up in the details of it being perfect, or of other people's opinions -- they just act. I come up with concepts all day every day. I then create a visual image for this "money generating mechanism" I have come up with and then I bring it to market. I don't care about who likes it or who doesn't. I don't care about who thinks it will work or will not work. I simply take action and bring it to market. Some of my ideas are "multi-million dollar ideas" and some of the them are complete flops. I don't care. With enough action I will make it work. Too many people spend too much time thinking and researching or dreaming and talking. Monsters "commit and watch creativity follow."

I can't tell you how many people have told me, "I can't believe you have your own TV show." I normally say, "Some talk, we do." One clear difference between the dreamer and the Monster is that the Monster sees it and does it. They may make mistakes along the way. They may have to occasionally re-calibrate. However, at least they are in the arena making things happen while others sit on the sidelines and are unwilling to make the phone calls, do the traveling, get uncomfortable, pay the price, or make things happen.

I'm always reminded of the quote from U.S. President Theodore Roosevelt when it comes to talking vs. doing.

"It is not the critic who counts; not the man who points out how the strong man stumbles, or where the doer of deeds could have done them better. The credit belongs to the man who is actually in the arena, whose face is marred by dust and sweat and blood, who strives valiantly; who errs and comes short again and again; because there is not effort without error and shortcomings; but who does actually strive to do the deed; who knows the great enthusiasm, the great devotion, who spends himself in a worthy cause, who at the best knows in the end the triumph of high achievement and who at the worst, if he fails, at least he fails while daring greatly. So that his place shall never be with those cold and timid souls who know neither victory nor defeat.

I meet so many people who want to write a book but they will not take the time to pump one out. They won't take Monster Action, they just have a Monster Mouth. They talk a good game but don't play a good game.

Steven Pressfield has become of my favorite authors. He wrote "The War of Art," "Turn Pro," and "Do the Work." I wish I had written these books. He talks about the difference between an amateur and a pro. You will know immediately when you listen to their language:

Amateur talk:

- I've always wanted to start my own business

- I've always dreamed of owning my own winery

- I've always wanted to travel the world

- I've always wanted to be a big star

Pros talk like this

- I'm starting my own business today

- I am acquiring my own winery

- I'm scheduling my travel around the world

- I'm in the process of becoming a big star and am willing to spend the money on the agent, marketing, and coaching I need to do it

I think it's important here to ask yourself a hard question. _Are you willing to do whatever it takes to manifest what you see in your mind?_ If not, then you can forget about being a Monster because a true Monster is a legendary creature. It's not a scaredy-cat. A true Monster embraces the work as opportunity, and is willing to wake up early or stay up late to outlast the competition. A true Monster is willing to be uncomfortable but to work through it.

Here is a list of common excuses, which are nothing more than _self-proclaimed opt-out clauses_ a non-Monster uses to skirt around the real truth – which is that they simply aren't willing to put the work in:

1. It will take too long.

2. It will cost too much.

3. It will be too hard.

4. I'm too old to get started.

5. I'm too young to get started.

6. Somebody else already owns the market.

7. I'm not smart enough.

8. I don't have the resources.

9. I don't have the time.

10. When they give me this or that, then I'll start.

This is Monster bull shit. The reality is if you use any of these excuses then you don't have what it takes in the tank to take the massive levels of action required to be the Monster you say you wish to become.

I see people get on social media and say they want to use it as a tool to promote their businesses but then they post to it one time per week. Perhaps they'll write one blog per month. Then they say, "I don't have the time to fool with it." In reality, all non-performers have is time. You have to get rid of all these excuses and remember that "anytime you think the problem is out there, this very thought is the problem."

Many people want to take action but don't know what actions to take. Here is a formula for the Monster:

Highest use of my time + my best strategies toward my dominant aspiration = realization of what I've always wanted.

If you're in the sales business, 80% of your day should be in money-generating activity. You should put a sign right in front of you that says, "Are you doing a money generating activity right now? If not, stop what you are doing."

Monster focus plus Monster Action in the key areas multiplies results.

Let's stop right here and do an activity inventory of how you are currently spending your time. Write down 5 things you do in a day. Then ask yourself, 'are they in the wheelhouse of what I should be doing to multiply my business?'

1. _____

2. _____

3. _____

4. _____

5. _____

Cull out everything you shouldn't be doing and focus only on taking Monster Action in the key areas that will multiply your business. A full 80% of your day should be spent in areas of the highest use of your time.

I'm working right now to cut out everything that is not moving me toward our ultimate aspiration. Remember this question: "Is what I'm doing moving me closer to my dominant aspiration?" If not, you don't need to be doing it.

Take a moment now and cull out at least five things you no longer need to be doing:

1. _____

2. _____

3. _____

4. _____

5. _____

Now write down the five most important things you need to be doing every single day to accelerate your path to where you want to be:

1. _____

2. _____

3. _____

4. _____

5. _____

Grant Cardone, author of the 10X rule, is dead-on right when it comes to this one. There are four levels of action that people take. Give yourself a grade on where you currently are:

1. Retreat - you are in a retreating mindset of scarcity and all of your action is contracting.

2. Do nothing - you are taking no action in your life and are totally reactive to whatever happens to you.

3. Normal - you are not doing anything extraordinary when it comes to action. You are taking the same level of action as most of those around you offering no differential advantage when it comes to effort.

4. Massive - you are multiplying the action you take to uncommon levels. You are not a common creature. You are a legendary creature that combines multiple skill sets to dominate a market.

The Monster takes Monster actions. It's just that simple. Other people will say things like "you need balance in your life," "you work too hard," or "how did you get where you are in life?" The reality is very few will take the kind of action it takes to be great, but there is a sliver of the population who are motivated by progress and mastery. They take the necessary action it takes to win at the highest levels.

The concept of "intentional congruence" is a new concept that combats the concept of balance. Right now I'm in Napa Valley, CA enjoying the beautiful mountains at one of the top resorts for relaxation in the world. I'm also writing this book, spending time with my wife, listening to podcasts, reviewing my 2019 goals, sitting by the pool, exercising, riding bikes, and eating great food.

I don't have to just "relax," or "work." My work can be relaxing. My time away can be re-juvenating and fruitful. Too many people get caught up in the concept of balance only to be off-balance in a LAZY WAY producing nothing.

God worked six straight days before he took a day off when he created the heavens and the earth. Most work too little, take off too much, and produce nothing extra-ordinary.

Intentional congruence means this:

I create a life that includes businesses and concepts I create that tie in to that life. I enjoy combining inspiration and execution therefore we created our retreat division so we could combine coaching and re-juvenation in cool places around the world.

Intentional congruence is where all facets of my business feed each other meaning:

My Monster Producer business feeds my retreat business.

My Monster Producer business feeds my real estate investments division called "The Revolution Group" as many of my investors come from Monster Producer.

My Monster Producer business feeds my friendships as many of my closest friends come from the program.

My Monster Producer business feeds my lifestyle meaning we create community and "exchange" ideas and energy with each other.

Intentional congruence is where it's at. Build a life a business where all parts of your life feeds all parts of your life.

One thing to note here as well is that many don't know the level of action it takes to create this life. I assume that when Nick Saban took over as head coach of the then struggling University of Alabama football team, the first thing he did was enlighten his new team to the kind of Monster action it would take to win a national championship. Those players only knew what they had been doing prior to Saban's arrival and the kind of results they got back in return back then. *They had not experienced new levels of action*. When many people enter our Monster Producer program they quickly find out that the level of action they are taking daily is NO WHERE near enough to become a Monster. Their frequency is too low. Their actions are too minimal. Their mindset is too small. We have to expand this and the only way to expand this is to "enlighten them" to a new way of thinking and doing business at at higher frequency.

When you lose, don't ever lose as a consequence of not taking action.

There are people you need to call right now. There are steps you need to be making. There are actions that need to be taken. There are decisions that need to be made. You don't have to be great to start but you'll never be great until you do! Draw a line in the sand right now and eliminate all the excuses that you and your team have been making that have limited your bigger futures. Don't allow small and limited action steps creep into your organization.

One of my favorite topics we cover in Monster Producer is the concept of "How to ask without consideration." A consideration is an "internal thought" that prohibits an action.

A consideration is something you think that prohibits you from making that call, starting that business, following up, or believing something will work. That consideration would come from:

- Your own insecurity

- Your own past failures

- Your own projections on to others

- Your own fear of rejection

- Your own tiny thinking

A consideration/hesitation prohibits you from:

- Calling on a strategic partner to do business together

- Following up on a proposal

- Calling on people in your Farm Club that you need to close

- Bringing solutions to bigger clients

- Starting something new until you have more information

- Going from a baby star to a big star

Take a moment now and write out all of the CONSIDERATIONS you operate from:

Regular Energy vs. Monster Energy

There's an energy drink called "Monster." It amps you up to un-ordinary levels of energy.

I once had Jon Gordon, author of "The Energy Bus" on my radio show and he made a strong statement that I'll never forget. He said, "In any given day, you will meet an enormous amount of negative energy. Your positive energy must be greater than any negative energy you will encounter."

This is Monster Energy. It's an insatiable desire backed by an unparalleled commitment to see an idea through to its logical conclusion.

It's not just being amped up. *It's being amped up with purpose.* It's not just throwing haymakers. It's the sweet science of boxing. It's movement with purpose. It's understanding that your batteries are storehouses of energy that can either be compounded or depleted.

My theory is simple: Every day that you wake up, you bring a certain amount of energy to the table based on the amount of rest, focus, resilience, food, etc. that you have chosen for your life. Like a cell phone battery, that energy tank begins to deplete throughout the day and can be completely drained from negative energy, or, like a cell phone recharging, it can also be compounded by positive energy.

The Monster is protective of his energy. He or she deploys it with people and in the right situations to conserve it for pivotal moments. Monsters place themselves in situations to have extended periods of high-end energy. They are the catalyst that starts the fire. They are the energy that wakes up the dead. They are the energy that brings to life an old and dying opportunity.

Lots of Monsters have others "suck" off the hind tit of their energy so they have to "energy up." If you plan on being this Monster, then you've got to realize the clear differences between regular levels of energy and superhuman energy. It has to do with this formula:

1. I am aware of what level of energy I create every day (low, medium, high, superhuman).

2. I know how to conserve my energy only for the right people and the right opportunities.

3. I say no to opportunities that "drain my battery" and obligate me to things I'm not passionate about.

4. I am a Monster and I am fully aware that many times I can win on ENERGY alone. This is controlled by me and I nourish my

storehouse of energy and never let it be depleted.

Think like this and remember the four levels of action:

1. Retreat and contract.

2. Do nothing.

3. Take normal levels of action with normal levels of energy.

4. Take Monster levels of action due to the Monster tank
   I'm carrying.

If you're going to be a MEGA MONSTER you've got to bring a whole new level of energy to the equation and become overly protective of your awareness of the energy you expel in a day.

For years I looked at people who operated at low frequencies of energy as being "lazy" until I met Monster Dr. Steven Hotze, founder of the Hotze Health and Wellness Center in Houston, TX. Through a coaching assignment with him he begin to educate me on how the body operates and I came to some big realizations about Monsters and their energy. He taught me this:

- As the body ages it naturally declines

- This decline shows itself in the form of the body not producing things it needs to be successful that produce energy

- Without these necessary things such as testosterone, thyroid, and other key elements individuals become tired and irritable

- This fatigue causes a lack of motivation and drive

- A person ends up losing his VEMM and VIGOR to pursue big goals and dominant aspirations

I began attending Dr. Hotze's Wellness Center as a guest to only find out that I was low in THYROID and TESTOSTERONE, key elements I needed to pursue the Monster goals I have. As I began adding to these minus the use of pharmaceutical drugs I began regaining the energy I needed. Dr. Hotze believes pharmaceutical drugs are toxins that pollute the body. Everything he does is to try and get you on a path to health and wellness minus these drugs so your body is prepared to accomplish the things you envision in your mind.

Because of this new revelation I now recommend that all Monsters see Dr. Hotze to get their levels right. No amount of motivation or internal drive will be able to compensate for your body not producing the proper levels it needs to pursue big dreams.

In my opinion the energy you need comes from two places:

1. A deep connection to your purpose

2. Your body operating at the levels it was meant to (An offensive posture)

The Monster who "burns out" has lost all joy and passion for his work really indicating:

1. He has lost connection to his purpose

2. His body, mind, and heart are fatigued prohibiting him from pursuit of a dominant focus.

My energy comes from this cycle:

1. I have had a big REVELATION: I was put on this earth to coach and develop the talent in others

2. Because of my REVELATION I now have CONVICTION: A deep seated confidence that I transfer to others to instill my confidence in to them

3. Because of this CONVICTION I take high frequency actions: This is the level of action required to produce at the highest levels.

Add the correct levels of energy produced by the regiment of:

1. Proper Exercise- I box 4X weekly, walk daily, and exercise in other forms

2. Proper Eating Diet- Dr. Hotze recommends the KETOGENIC diet

3   Replacement of correct hormones in the body- To get the body back to its intended state

4. Vitamins and supplements- Areas to increase energy daily

I remember a 55 year old Christian book writer who wanted me to coach her on how to take her book to the market. I outlined all of the things I felt like she needed to do which included:

- A book tour

- Podcasts

- Blogs

- Speaking Engagements

- Book launch parties

- The use of a selling and marketing system

She looked at me and said a statement I'll never forget, "I don't have the energy to do all of those things."

I wrote down on my note pad this statement:

I never want to be in a position where my health and energy levels prohibit me from taking the level of action I need to be successful and to impact the world.

Take a moment now and write out your REVELATION, CONVICTION, and ACTIONS you will be taking after reading this chapter.

CHAPTER 4

MONSTER FRAMEWORK #4 CULTIVATE "MONSTER NETWORKS"

"Monsters have deep and entrenched networks of key players who can get things done at a moment's notice. They activate these networks by learning the art and skill of creating unique value for those networks and deep advocating for other people in a systematic manner." To build a deep network you must create something of deep value where people are pursuing you. You are the "buyer vs. the seller." You are a "Person of Interest."

I just returned from Las Vegas and speaking at Brad Lea's LightSpeed Virtual Training summit with some of the biggest names in the world. Five years ago I didn't know Brad Lea. By being associated with Grant Cardone I met Brad who then introduced me to other big time players. By speaking at 10X I met Ed Mylett, Tim Storey, Tim Grover, and many more. This is how you expand your network. Let's go back to that hard skill again. It was the hard skill that got me on the stages and afforded me the ability to get to know other big time players. Many people get networking confused as some low level activity of talking to strangers and handing out business cards. We network to "compliment" each other. We each bring unique skills to the equation that play nicely with others. When we combine these talents there is greater synergy.

To become a Monster you have to let go of the considerations you have like, "I'm not good enough to be in the same room with those people," or "I'll never run with that crowd."

All of these are insecurities.

When you work for a decade on your hard skill and get affirmation from the market that the world needs what you've got it is then time to take that skill to the masses by connecting with influencers. Remember, they are just people like you are. They want and need what you have. It's just a matter of getting over your fears and asking to partner with them.

I've now become good friends with some of the top performance people in the world. I'm doing retreats with them where I'm spending four uninterrupted days with them in a relaxed setting. I'm partnering with them in my virtual training platform.

Remember, we can't network until we create some kind of value for others that they want and need. Handing a person a business card is not value. Creating revenue for them is a value. Bringing something to the equation they currently don't have is a value. Adding an asset to their life is a value.

First work on you to become a "Person of Interest" so they see the confidence and value in you and want to partner with you.

Every Monster has a wide range of people or "deep network" that they can call on. There is a systematic way to build deep and entrenched networks of power players, feeder systems, and multiplier relationships with a specific mindset to help them advance their strategy first with the value you create. To become a Monster you must advance and expand on this empire of connections. Too few people try to sell and exchange with too few of people. If you have a network of just a few it's hard to advance a big dream.

This is important. Lots of people believe that you build networks by going to networking events and handing out business cards. The Monster builds deep networks by creating unique and propriety value that nobody else brings to the party. Other people need what you have. It's just a matter of exposing them to the value that you create that they didn't know about. This is what "networking is." Monster are true experts in their space that others seek out and want to spend time with. They are _buyers v. sellers_, meaning people come to them vs. them going to others. They are "people of interest" in whom the market finds deep value in. This ties back to the "hard skill" we discussed in the beginning of this book. You possess something attractive.

In the old days, Dale Carnegie taught us to be "interested" vs. "interesting." **The Monster is both**. They are deeply interested in their network's success but they are also deeply interesting and others find them incredibly valuable to their businesses and lives.

They are challengers v. pure relationship builders. Their results get serious attention from the market and they spend a great deal of time challenging those in their networks and helping them drive their dominant aspirations while simultaneously creating a skill set that others find fascinating.

Many people are simply not self-aware enough to step back from their lives and see what makes them interesting. They just go along and get along never developing the breadth and depth they really need to become the dominant player in the market or to become the Monster go-to player. They take normal levels of action as it relates to building their skill set, which is common, not unique.

Bishop T.D. Jakes once said, "That which is common many times is considered cheap. That which is rare is considered valuable." To cheapen anything, just make it common. To drive up value, by comparison, just make it rare. We should constantly be evaluating what makes us unique and differentiating to the market. What makes a monster special is their unique background of experiences, thought processes, successes and failures.

The Monster builds deep networks first by finding and cultivating something that is rare and valuable in the market and then by figuring out who would see the most interest in it. Last, they use their skill sets to add creative value to others while combining their craft with the go-giver mindset.

Monster Drill:

1. My unique skill set is _____
   _____ and I create unique and proprietary
   value in the form of knowledge, expertise, products, or services,
   which is _____
   _____.

2. The three most fascinating parts of my life that are of value to
   those in my networks are:

   a. _____

   b. _____

   c. _____

3. My top three strategies for creating real value for my network
   this coming year are (Think of new and differentiated value):

   a. _____

   b. _____

   c. _____

Value creation by the Monster most likely stems from each individuals' unique past, which is packaged up into unique processes or systems that other people need and can use immediately. Think of weaving each of your unique experiences into that which makes you valuable to the market.

While cruising through the eastern Caribbean on a business cruise with my friend Clayton Whitaker, a successful Monster it didn't take long for me to realize where his real value was. Raised by a Baptist preacher and car expert, Clayton started in the banking and lending business. Reading and studying the work of Stephen Covey, combined with Grant Cardone's 10X mentality, we ended up with this:

A former banker who has a big heart, who was great with numbers, and had the drive of a massive-level thinker, Whitaker combined these unique skills to create Dealer Capital Services, a firm that buys loans at small car dealerships to provide necessary capital for the dealers to purchase more inventory, pay down debt, and build their businesses. His rich background and human interest instilled in him by his father made him compassionate to all and his business savvy prompted him to want to dominate his markets and the world for that matter. Clayton can use these "unique skills" to create "unique processes" that can be monetized.

Take a moment and think through these things:

1. My unique past is:

2. My unique mentors were:

3. My unique skills are:

4. My unique talents help:

5. My unique processes solve these problems:

Monsters get paid by advancing the needs of others through their skill sets. They wake up and add Monster levels of value to others through creativity, relationships, direction, and confidence. They create energy and synergistic relationships by getting lost in other people's dreams in ways others cannot replicate. They build a moat around those they value so they never even think of turning to anybody else. They constantly think about how they can continue down the path of value creation in unique ways and they love sharing with people in their networks. They don't hoard information, they are free with it. One important part of networking is the "free prize," a unique add on or plus one that no one else creates. It's an in addition to concept.

My good friend Dr. Hotze spends a great deal of time sending framed pictures, signed books, and video messages to his new guests, people he meets, and friends to add value to their lives. When Dr. Hotze visited Nashville, TN and offered a speaking engagement to the Monsters he took time to take pictures with my bus driver Teddy Taylor and sent them back to him with a personal note. It made a lasting impression on Teddy.

The Monster also uses a series of tactics and strategies to get lost in other people's dreams. It looks like this:

1. Constancy of purpose by staying involved in the lives of others in a consistent and ongoing manner (see my Top 25 in the next chapter).

2. Constant "pinging" or touching base with those in their networks to show they care, especially in times of need, struggle, or celebration.

3. Showcase or activation events they combine and invite their networks too.

4. Thorough analysis and understanding of other people's businesses so they can create value, add value, and refer on a consistent basis.

5. The "inclusion concept" where they constantly think of ways to include their networks in everything important that they do.

6. A mindset that says this, "Whatever we do, let's do it together."

7. A mindset of gratitude for the value your network partners create and an awareness of when they need your attention.

Most people remember birthdays and anniversaries. This is not close enough on an "effort scale" to build a deep and entrenched "Monster Network." You have to do the inconvenient. To create unique value, stay at the top of people's minds with frequency of touch and motion. Show that you bring something incredibly unique and valuable to the party. Take a moment right now and decide which five ways you will include your networks in your life:

1. _____

2. _____

3. _____

4. _____

5. _____

In the "Current of the Urgent," we note that the speed and frequency in which the world is now coming at people can be overwhelming. They are simply overloaded and don't have time for many small or unnecessary gestures that most do to build networks (handwritten cards, post cards, birthday cards, etc.) Monsters "move the needle" with their networks by creating real value that someone can take and use immediately. They are "immediate assets" to others by building this mindset that a network is incredibly valuable to building a successful and meaningful life and healthy business.

To build Monster Networks, ***think Monster Unique Value***. Ordinary levels of value do not create movement in another's life. It's the equivalent of a gnat that annoys v. a true advocate that adds.

CHAPTER 5

MONSTER FRAMEWORK #5 UTILIZE A "MONSTER SELLING SYSTEM" TO CREATE REVENUE

"90% of people we work with have fewer than three strategies to acquire a customer. In today's saturated and commoditized world, this never even scratches the surface to get the number of leads they need to hit their sales targets." We believe you need to stack strategies on top of each other to drive up the probability of increasing sales.

At 31 years old and after I had written four books I decided to retire from athletic coaching and start a coaching business. That business was initially called "Maximum Success." It was a coaching and consulting business and most of my clients were corporations who wanted me to come in and coach their people toward some dominant aspiration, typically related to revenue production.

This was an uncertain time in my young business life. I didn't have a way to generate leads or business and quickly figured out I needed one. I got all the common business advice like "Call 100 people per week," "join the local chamber," and "Get your name out there." None of these were real strategies. My only strategy back then was get in front of any group that had a pulse and be so dynamic I got a few referrals from the room and took the one time speaking engagement and turned it into a coaching contract.

As the years went by, I got tired of chasing business. I got tired of handing out business cards and going to chamber events. Calling 100 people per week (frankly) sucked and was for the birds.

As a result, I created a true "selling system," a systematic way to plan my weeks around the highest use of my time married with my best customer-getting strategies that was in alignment with my dominant focus (the tangible outcome you would like to drive in a 12-month cycle as measured in 30-day windows). This system became known as **Legacy Selling**, a selling system to dramatically increase the probability of selling through both unique positioning, activation events, and relationship selling where you plan, execute, and circulate with purpose on a daily basis in alignment with where you need to go. We get crystal clarity around the "highest use of our time" married to our best strategies to actually get the phone to ring with a qualified buyer on the other end.

The great social ecologist Peter Drucker summed up the purpose of any business, which was "to create a customer." The problem comes when you spend so much time working "on the business" that you don't have enough time to work "in the business." Working "on the business" consists of specific and intentional activity to serve customers or improve the business. Working "in the business" represents specific and intentional time to get more customers.

Many people are skewed working "on the business." Monsters never forget that the purpose of any business is to create more customers. They balance their time between getting customers and servicing customers, and between creating interest and buzz in the market and building better processes and systems.

The Monster has a plan that includes both "lead" indicators, those activities you intentionally plan on doing at the beginning and throughout the week, and "lag" indicators, a recap of which strategies actually worked and which ones need to be re-calibrated. It is the combination and collusion of all of these strategies working together that helps drive up more leads, create more opportunity, and close more deals.

Every week, the Monster Producer maps out their week in their Monster Planner around these strategies as part of the Legacy Selling System:

1. Hit List – a minimum of 10 people weekly that you believe you can "help" with your services and who fit in the box of the ideal client you want on your client list. Your HIT LIST can consist of four distinct places:

   1. Current clients you are calling to extract referrals

   2. Past clients you are following up with after the transaction

   3. Strategic partners who you need to be exchanging ideas and business with

   4. Direct leads created by using this system

2. Farm Club - as many people as you can get who have indicated genuine interest in your services by giving you an IOI (indicator of interest). You are farming these people to get them to close and need a minimum of seven "unique" touches to get them to close. 'Maybes' do you no good here. You push people to a buying decision. We teach a concept of seven great touches when a person indicates interest and you will know of that interest within the first 15 seconds of you sharing your "Explanation of Services." The touches should be a combo of both "linear" or straight line and specific and "non-linear" or softer touches that cause a person to think and respond. You will want to pick up a copy of my book "Million Dollar Follow Up" to understand how we challenge the prospect to bring them to a buying decision.

3. Top 25 – Twenty-five deep and meaningful relationships with people who can refer and advocate for you that you love working with and bring you energy vs. drain your energy. By using the Monster Network philosophy, you create and add unique value to these peoples' lives through high-touch relationships and high-frequency contact. This is where your deep referral partners come in and make you lots of money. We believe that to build long term loyalty you need to focus on your top 1% of your clients expecting 3-6 referrals per year out of this group of people. We also believe you can make a million extra dollars or more per year

out of your TOP 25. Think of this group as your "PRESIDENTIAL LEVEL" and they get unique access to you, high touch and high frequency, exclusive access to your product or service, and access to other TOP 25 MEMBERS for exchange between them. Each week I target 3 of my top 25 and spend valuable time with them. You may even create various levels of engagement like we have with our basic level of Monster Producer, our $25K Level, and our Monster Tycoon level. This gives your clients the ability to climb up the ladder, engage with you at a deeper level, and have expanded products and services.

4. Connectors - Two meetings per week with "influencers," or those who can "connect" you to their Monster Networks. You bring value -- they have value. You offer them yours in exchange for access to their networks. Too few people understand this strategy. Think of it this way, we are all just one person away from a new season in life. Sometimes it takes this that one introduction or that one advocate to open the door to possibility for you. I target connectors and ask "who can open that door for me." Usually if I think hard enough I know someone based on my Monster Network that can open the door. When you learn to "ask without hesitation," a concept we teach in Monster you then will not be afaid to pick up that phone and make that call or schedule that meeting.

5. Unrelenting Advocates – a goal of taking your newly-signed customers and speeding up the referral faster by creating an experience that lends itself to quick referrals. There is a clear difference between a satisfied customer and an unrelenting advocate and there must be an experience that includes three unique "wows" as part of the customer experience. The best time to ask for a referral is ANY TIME but specifically at the "highest points of energy" which are always in the BEGINNING of any relationship. I teach my sales team that they should be working people in the first 30-60-90 days of the new relationship to ask for new business. Ask this way, "We believe like gravitate toward like and association breeds assimilation. We have loved

working with you and know we would love working with your friends." Asking for a referral from an unrelenting advocate should be easy as they are already on board with you due to the better state you have gotten them in to. When you take their low thoughts of value and convert them to high thoughts of value and also bring clarity to their confusion they will want to bring new people to the party. What you don't want to do is build a "passive experience" which means a lukewarm experience that they can take or leave in the future. These people will never fight for you.

6. Climbers - Identifying two people per week who are on the "fast track" and could be a valuable partner or client now and even more valuable in the future (or those who can't do business today but can at some point in the future).

7. Showcase/Activation Events - Planning a minimum of one-to-two showcase events per month where you strategically bring people together and offer them unique value. You do this through relationships, instilling confidence and energy, and providing networks – all of which positions you as the true expert in the market. You create these events for exposure (see next chapter), energy, and compounding energy. This is actually one of my best strategies as I constantly look for ways to bring people together to deepen bonds and deepen relationships. You can host entertainment showcase events, education showcase events, or edutainment showcase events that combine education and entertainment (Just add WINE and you'll see what I mean).

8. Database - Weekly or monthly, you create and share important and key information with your fans and stakeholders that adds to their lives vs. subtracts from them. This content either appeals to the niches or appeals to the masses but is not the common trash most people send out solely so they can cross it off the list and feel like they did something. If it's not interesting, don't send it. It only clutters the e-mails of already cluttered inboxes and frustrates the end user. I personally write all of the e-mails that go

to my database, specifically the ones on content as I want people to read them. Bring value, not spam. Have a message. Have a pont of view. Have a message that either repels or attracts. Don't have a lukewarm message you can't build loyalty behind. People won't read or get behind people who say something boring.

9. Social Media - The Monster works hard to use this free medium to become the celebrity in their space. They create an identity around their interesting point of view and focus on five core areas:

   a. Content - They have a breadth and depth that is deep and wide.

   b. Delivery - Frequency is high to stay at the top of people's minds.

   c. Position - They have a clear and concise philosophy others can easily identify with.

   d. Packaging - The way they are packaged drives up the value of their offering v. drives it down.

   e. Multipliers - They attract large groups of people by being interesting. The opposite of interesting is disinteresting or boring.

10. Podcast - Monsters use every social media tool they can to share their knowledge. They create a weekly podcast to share their knowledge base and open other doors followers and fans can enter through. Every Monster needs their own podcast to share their POV (point of view) and distribute their content to the world through multiple mediums.

11. Videos/TV - Monsters either create their own TV show on traditional TV or on YouTube or Vimeo that offers an additional medium for people to get to know them and acclimate with them. I create weekly shows like "Super Coach," "Person of Interest," "Living with a Monster," and "Monster Producer" as a way to connect with people in a consistent manner that helps to build affinity with a market of people and attract new people.

These 11 strategies create energy. They create movement. They create attention. They create activity. And money always follows these four things.

The opposite of the Monster is the "secret agent," the sales person who hides out in his office hoping the phone rings and relies on static websites, traditional media sources, and past customers to fuel their future business.

Monsters never let "old confidence turn into new ignorance." Monsters are constantly looking to create synergy between multiple strategies to drive up interest in the market. Monsters attack the week v. have the week attack them. Monsters wake up on fire and create such a volume of activity that the market cannot deny them.

Monsters go out and make the world go round. From the 11 strategies that are part of the Legacy Selling System take a moment now and write out which of these strategies you plan on using to generate new interest:

CHAPTER 6

MONSTER FRAMEWORK #6 YOU MUST GET "MONSTER EXPOSURE" FOR YOU AND YOUR BUSINESS (MONEY FOLLOWS ATTENTION)

"The number one challenge of every business owner on the planet is not that they are not incredibly good. It's that nobody knows who the hell they are."

As you know I speak all over the country and many times people walk up to me with a wonderful compliment that looks like this, "We have seen ALL of the personal growth and sales people in the world speak and you are just as good as they are." This is a complement but one that drives me crazy. If I am as good as they are then why are they commanding 10X the money that I am? The difference between them and me many times is eyeballs, meaning they have a bigger "following" than I do. I believe "attention equals dollars" and that people who are the most known get the most opportunity. Part of our job as Monsters is to get more attention. This is hard for many because they were raised "not to get attention." For some strange reason they don't want to "promote" their services to other people.

Currently me and my investors are spending roughly $7,500 per month in marketing to buy ads on Facebook and Instagram. Add $3,000+ per month in advertising, and more for click funnels. This is the cost of doing business to become known in the world. If you only become known to a very small group of people you don't have any new people to sell to. You just sell to the same people. Part of us opening up new markets through certified coaches is to expand our message. Part of me purchasing the airplane last year was to be able to spread my message faster and to more people on Planet

Earth. Until you become "known" or famous in your market you're obscure and you can only help a few people like this.

Monsters have a desire to become KNOWN in their space. They want attention for their work. They KNOW this is the only way they can really do some serious damage in the world through their work.

The Monster is savvy in branding, positioning, and leveraging a following of "lil' monsters" that are interested in being in his or her mix. The "exposure strategies" the Monster wields involve cultivating a unique "monster" point of view that attracts massive, engaged followers of fans and people who resonate with them and their philosophy.

When it comes to being a business owner, whether big or small, many think their predominant problem is that they just don't have the capital to expand. I think their initial problem is even bigger than that – and that problem is obscurity.

To be a Monster, you've got to get Monster attention. You've got to get large numbers of eyeballs on you and your product. You have to cut through the noise and clutter of weaker brands to consistently have high touch and high frequency in the back of people's minds because in those minds is a tiny piece of real estate and on that piece of real estate is somebody else that also does what you do. The question then becomes, how do YOU own that real estate, so much so that you literally dominate the thoughts of others even when they don't want you to?

Here are some principles to remember when seeking to get attention for your business:

1. Don't watch the news, create the news.

2. Take that which is common and make it uncommon.

3. Take that which is ordinary and make it extraordinary.

4. Break patterns.

5. Lose your filter.

6. Be the first in the market doing something.

7. Be the most unique in the market doing something.

8. Be the most vocal in the market.

9. Position yourself as the most controversial or most active.

Monsters crave attention. By comparison, insecure people hide. How much attention should you be getting? I believe you should be getting weekly, daily, and minute-by-minute attention. Remember what money follows. It follows attention, energy, movement, and action. It does not follow boredom, retreat, contraction, or insecurity.

To get this attention, we have to look at what everybody else is doing and do the polar opposite. The opposite in our language. The opposite in our branding. The opposite in our marketing. And the opposite in our offerings.

The opposite of interesting is boring, but interesting is not enough. We have to become fascinating. We have to become over the top. We have to become "Freaking Monsters."

Let's look at some specific things I've done to get attention:

1. Set out to break a world record (executing the most speaking engagements in one day).

2. Purchased and wear a Zebra print jacket when I speak.

3. Partner with controversial people and utilize their platforms.

4. Push big parties as customer activation events.

5. Push my message hard through social media daily and weekly.

6. Take a stance on tough issues that either attract or repel.

7. Use challenger tactics to push people to take action vs. allow them to control the scenario.

8. Blast markets with a barrage of marketing collateral: signs, events, banners, newspaper articles, direct mail pieces, radio campaigns and more.

9. Created a new reality TV show.

10. Created a podcast.

11. Created a weekly TV show on YouTube.

12. Pushed out a database hit every single week.

13. Write a weekly blog for the local newspaper.

14. Host themed New Year's Eve parties.

Here's the main point. You want more attention for your business, not less. You want more people talking about you, not less. You want that buzz about your business to go WILD.

In 2014, pop star Miley Cyrus put on a provocative show at the MTV music awards. Through bold, half-naked gestures, she created a national media storm for two weeks. This display just happened to come right before her documentary was coming out and her new album dropped.

Although you might not agree with her methodology, her stunt did the trick. Right out of the playbook of Lady Gaga and the original shocker, Madonna, these ladies have cultivated the ability to get massive amounts of attention.

The first things insecure people will say to me about this concept are:

1. If I get attention, people will talk about me (DUH? That's the buzz you want!)

2. My own colleagues will not like this if I break the mold and go against the grain (Do you want to be liked? Or do you want to win?)

3. I feel uncomfortable doing this (I know, you are expanding!)

4. I don't know what to do (Yes you do, you just don't have the "you-know-what" to do it.)

Monsters are "legendary creatures" that combine multiple skill sets to dominate the market. When asked what makes Tony Robbins so good or what made Steve Jobs so successful, many of the people close to them have said the exact same thing, "They are brilliant marketers." They have products just like everybody else. They simply become better marketers than everybody else.

You know you have the goods. You know you are the best in your market, possibly even the world. What you have to do now is get the word out about what you've got. And in the "current of the urgent," you have to get it out early and often. You have to beat the drum incessantly to cut through the noise and clutter of other weaker brands. You have to draw attention and energy to you.

Larry Winget, "The Pitbull of Personal Development," was just a regular ol' motivational speaker until one day while on stage he got tired of feeding people the same old bull shit that everybody else was feeding them. While being heckled from the audience, Winget looked at his assaulter and said, "Your life is your own damn fault."

This was the beginning of a new Larry, "The Pitbull," with the wild shirts and boots and a no-holds-barred mindset of saying what nobody else would say. He went on to be a multi-millionaire, have his own TV show, and write multiple best-selling books because he went in a different direction from all the other motivational speakers of his time that focused exclusively on the positive and spoke mainly in platitudes about what a person could become.

Now, it's time to put together you're Monster Exposure plan:

1. What will you say that is different from what everybody else in your industry is saying?

2. How will you create a distinct look from everybody else in your industry?

3. What will be your top three to five strategies to get attention on a consistent basis for your business?

4. What is rare and most valuable about your business?

5. How will you position yourself differently from everybody else?

6. What specific changes do you need to make to your marketing and advertising right now?

7. What three tactics will you try to get massive amounts of attention for this quarter?

8. What events will you create to pull people together so you can be seen as the expert in your space?

9. What new concept will you bring to the market that solves a problem that you will get attention for?

10. What part of this Monster Exposure causes you the most anxiety and what's your biggest obstacle?

Remember, Monsters are Monsters for a reason. They are not interested in remaining small. They want to dominate and are willing to do what it takes to get the necessary attention and to draw massive amounts of people and eyeballs to them.

As I evaluate my business in 2018 it's clear to me of my missing structures including:

1. An agent who has national and international connections to connect me and get me on the biggest stages in the world

2. A marketing engine to go from getting 250,000 views to 2 million views

3. An aggressive sales arm making outbound calls for our products and services

Take a moment now and highlight the areas that you are deficient as it relates to getting more attention for your business. My guess is this:

You don't have a message that is strong enough.

You don't share that message with enough people.

You are not spending any money on marketing or advertising.

Your website looks like everyone else and you don't understand click funnels and new strategy to build new clients.

You are not using a selling system to become better known in the market.

You are still using old marketing plays or replicating what you see other people do in your space.

You are not generating enough buzz through social or showcases.

You are not using your database to build a tribe and connect with that tribe on a consistent basis.

Circle the areas you need the most work in and remember this, "You can't sell a secret." Part of being a Monster is the CONVICTION and DRIVE to take your message to a bigger world. It will require that you LEAVE the comfort of being liked and the comfort of being known to a small group of people and expand that to many more people. For every 350 people you share your message with the Law of Diffusion and Innovation tells me that less than 52.8 will be interested quickly.

CHAPTER 7

MONSTER FRAMEWORK #7
BUILD A "MONSTER ENTERPRISE" THAT SERVES YOUR LIFE AND YOUR VISION- THE GOAL SHOULD BE TO SCALE YOUR BUSINESS

"Your business should be set up to "serve your Monster Life" vs. "run your life."

If you have followed my work for some time you've heard me say, "Long obedience in the same direction," and that I believe in "mastery" vs. "cotton candy." This is my way of saying that you have to "do the work" to move from an amateur to a professional. You can't scale chaos. You have to put the time in to build something that is ready to scale. You have to build the revenue you absolutely must have to make moves and hire more people. A business is designed before there is a business but I never designed my business properly in the beginning. I just went out in to the world and did my thing. I didn't think about the "design" of the business.

Monster Tycoon Tom Love said to me one day this statement, "You're going to practice everything you preach and go out in to the market and create so much business that you're going to hate it." I laughed but he was exactly right. I was adding more engagements, more commitments, more people, and never stepped back and designed a business I could scale. Most just go out and try and generate revenue. They don't think about design of the business or scaling the business or what happens when they run out of gas running that successful business.

Now, everything I do is toward scaling my enterprise. I want to build my business where I wake up daily and do exactly what I want to do.

I want to produce enough revenue to generate excess cash that can then be re-invested in my own business, other deals, and real estate plays that bring me passive income.

Now, at 42 I'm trying to scale. This is why you seeing me push:

1) Certified Coaches

2) Online Academies

3) Higher levels of coaching

4) Monster in a Box

5) Retreats (that others even execute)

6) Licensing

7) Building Greatness Factories and Greatness Factories for Kids

I wish I had coaching at 31 to teach me how to do this from the beginning, but I didn't.

Your business should serve your life, not run your life. It should produce money and energy, not suck your money and your energy. This chapter tells you how to build a Monster Enterprise.

Monster Mogul Derek Godwin made this statement one day, "When I entered Monster Producer I was spending 98% of my time involved in every aspect of running my business. Now I spend less than 2% running it."

This is how you build a Monster Enterprise.

The plight of the American small business owner often looks like this:

1. Work 60-80 hours per week

2. Never see family or friends

3. Be on call 365 days per year

4   Chase business

5. Struggle with hiring and firing employees

6. Become frustrated and agitated constantly

7. Break even or lose money month after month and have to borrow to make payroll

67% of all small business owners in American break even or lose money at the end of every month. Does this sound like success to you?

Of course not. It's time to become a Monster.

Your business should be set up to do some Monster things, such as:

1. Pay yourself what you think your real value is to the market.

2. Pay all of your expenses and investments you need to grow and scale the business.

3. Offer you plenty of money to pay your taxes with without straining your entire business.

4. Give you excess cash at the end of every month (10-20%) that you can re-invest in you, your passions, your future, or other money generating ideas.

5. Let you pick and choose when you work and what you work on v. being a slave to your business.

A Monster Business should "serve your life" vs. "run your life." After all, that's why you got into business to begin with, right?

In this chapter, I want to have you paint a picture of what a "Monster Life" looks like to you. As I write this, my ship is pulling in to port in the Bahamas in the midst of a seven-day cruise experience that I created years ago to marry my inspiration and execution together. I'm sitting on deck 8 looking out at a bay and an island in a completely relaxed and comfortable state. This week-long adventure has offered me the important opportunity to connect with new friends, speak and train (something I love to do), entertain and visit, and complete my 'bigger goals' list. All the while, I'm mixing work and play together.

This is called "Lifestyle Design," which is where your work serves your life vs. runs your life. While I've been in the Bahamas, my team of trusted advisors have still been working (leverage), books have been sold online (passive income), my investment properties have brought in more rent (passive income), my membership model is still serving clients (passive income), and my brand is still growing (new followers). We are on our way to building an "enterprise" vs. being a "solo-preneur." We do that by building multiple profit centers.

A solo-preneur is person who has an idea and pursues that idea and converts it into a viable business. Sometimes they become millionaires (mostly single digit) but many times it takes the leverage of others to help build an enterprise. It also takes "scalable" or "passive portfolios" to build multiple money streams that the entrepreneur is not always directly involved in.

Many times when I work with clients, they have one stream of income. I call this stream their "money vehicle" and unfortunately that vehicle cannot get them to their desired financial destination. They work hard for money v. working and designing a business that gives them freedom. With enough money, they can buy that time and freedom that they've always wanted.

Ask yourself this question before we proceed: Is my business vehicle set up to serve my life? Or run my life?

I remember one day stepping into a Dairy Queen to buy some ice cream. The owner/franchisee waited on me at the counter. I asked, "How are you enjoying owning this business?" He said, "It's awesome, I get to decide which 80 hours I work this week."

I don't think he gets the picture. We want to work because it helps to fulfill our dharma, or purpose in life, and is the distribution channel for our talents. We don't want to be in a position to have to work just to pay the bills and then do it all over again next week.

Author Kiyosaki calls this the "Rat Race" and says what we really want to get on is the "Fast Track." The "Fast Track" to what, you ask? The "Fast Track" of passive income by creating assets (that which makes us money whether we work or not) v. doing what most middle class people do, which is buy liabilities (that which takes money out of our pockets whether we work or not). One adds to our income, while the other subtracts from our income.

Kiyosaki also went on to define the "Cashflow Quadrant," or the four ways that every person derives their money. As you read this list, ask yourself, which one is the predominant way cash flows into your account?

1. Employee - you work for others.

2. Self-Employed - you work for yourself as a solo-preneur with a small business.

3. Big business - you have systems and structures that work for you and people (leverage).

4. Investor - you have your money working for you. Kiyosaki urges everyone to get out of the employee and self-employed philosophy, as this is where your time and energy are sucked dry by other people and where your small business may or may not be the vehicle that brings in enough cash to build your "Monster Life."

Now, let's take a moment and draw up the tenants of your "Monster Life."

My Monster Life looks like this:

1. I work this many days per week: _____

2. My salary for that work is: _____

3. The total revenue of my company is: _____

4. I live in this city: _____

5. I have a second or third home in these cities: _____

_____

6. I get to spend a portion of my time doing or following this passion:

_____

7. Most of my time at work is spent doing exactly what I love, which is

_____

8. My passive income is: _____

9. My multiple profit centers that brings in that passive income is:

_____

10. I no longer have to do this: _____

11. The Monster Project I'm working on right now is: _____

_____

12. In the next five years, I'm going to start a new enterprise I've always wanted to do, which is this: _____

_____

Who says you can't have it all? Who says you've got to live in the "Rat Race?" Who says you can't build a "Monster Business" that allows you to have a "Monster Life?"

One of the sayings I constantly utilize in my life and in my books is simple: Every action you take is driven by your thoughts and your thoughts are no wiser than your understandings. If you have little thoughts, they manifest themselves into little actions and you produce a little life.

That is the opposite of a Monster Life. Let's draw up the number of abilities you have that can be compensated in the market right now:

1. My Monster Ability is this: _____

_____

2. I can fill these gaps or holes in the market with my abilities:

_____

3. If I created three passive income streams TODAY, they would be:

   a. _____

   b. _____

   c. _____

4. I can envision myself creating these passive income streams in the future from my business:

   a. _____

   b. _____

   c. _____

5. My business can become the vehicle and revenue source I need it to be to create the Monster Life I envision. I just need to unlock the following "acres of diamonds" and fill these "missing structures" to do it:

   a. _____

   b. _____

   c. _____

There are more millionaires created in economic recessions than during any other time. The opportunity is abundant and is ready for the taking. You can build a "Monster Life" and your business can be the conduit to help you wake up every day and do exactly what you love while being compensated at exactly the high rate that you deserve.

The Monster Finish

I want to re-visit how we defined a Monster Producer in the beginning of this book. We said that a Monster was "A legendary creature that combines multiple skill sets to dominate a market." A Monster is a "Person of Interest." A Monster is a "Zebra and Cheetah." A Monster is a "Legacy Seller." A Monster has all the SWAG in the world. A Monster can pivot fast, build deep networks, add Monster Value, see and seize opportunity, create a massive business, and live a Monster Life.

We used to think of the word Monster as a negative creature. By contrast, I believe we need to build more Monsters in the world. They are truly the ones who dominate every space they are in.

Are you ready to become the Monster in your market?

Few wake up daily and want to dominate. Many wake up merely to compete. Most struggle to prosper and live an abundant life. Their lives are filled with minor frustrations and inconveniences vs. a life that gives life and meaning. A Monster Producer wakes up with something BIG inside of them. They have the energy and vision, they just need the right vehicle, the right platform, and the right exposure. Once these key elements are in place their lives and their businesses begin to take off.

From this point forward I want you to think of yourself as a MONSTER. You are no longer ordinary. You will no longer achieve ordinary outcomes, go to ordinary places, and accomplish ordinary dreams. You are going to fully utilize the talents God has given you. You are going to take dominion over your land and explode into the universe. Many people will want to have a relationship with you. Success won't be easy but it will come to you because you are becoming more attractive to the universe. You are now operating at a higher frequency with higher ordinance thinkers who want the best for you.

You are now part of the MONSTER NATION...

This is an international movement of like minded achievers.

Thank you for being a part of it!!

Are you an individual who wants to become a "Monster?" Learn more about our Monster Producer Coaching Program at monsterproducer.com.

- Do you want your sales people to become "Monster Producer?" Learn more about our Monster Producer Programs for companies and sales teams here: coachburt.com

Bring Coach Burt in to speak at your event by going to coachburt.com

We also do these things:

The Monster Nation Tour — A new kind of conference coming to a city near you

Monster Faith Events

Raising a Monster at The Greatness Factory for Kids

Living with a Monster with my wife Natalie Burt

Working for a MONSTER- The #1 and #2 Conference

Monster Teams

See Coach Burt train live or visit the original Greatness Factory at mygreatnessfactory.com.

OTHER BOOKS BY COACH BURT INCLUDE:

Everybody Needs a Coach in Life

Person of Interest

SWAG

Zebras and Cheetahs

Legacy Selling

Small Towns and Big Dreams

This Ain't No Practice Life

The Intangibles

CPSIA information can be obtained
at www.ICGtesting.com
Printed in the USA
JSHW040539110922
30263JS00003B/5

9 781732 788503